Anti-Bride Wedding Planner:

HIP TIPS & TOOLS FOR GETTING HITCHED

CAROLYN GERIN

KATHLEEN HUGHES

AMY GLYNN HORNICK

ILLUSTRATIONS BY ITHINAND TUBKAM AND CAROLYN GERIN

CHRONICLE BOOKS

SAN FRANCISCO

Text © 2004 Carolyn Gerin
Illustrations © 2004 Subset, Inc.

ISBN-10: 0-8118-4254-1
ISBN-13: 978-0-8118-4254-9
Design by Amy Ennis
Illustration concept by Carolyn Gerin and Ithinand Tubkam
Manufactured in China

10

Chronicle Books LLC
680 Second Street
San Francisco, CA 94107
www.chroniclebooks.com

Contents

Anti-Bride Thanks and Acknowledgments

Carolyn Gerin *For Laurent*—Croix de bois, croix de fer, si je mens, je vais en enfer. *For my mother*—*I think of you every day and feel you by my side. For my grandmother, Dorothy, my inspiration and benchmark for courage and moxie. For my father*—*you are my hero. For Kathleen, you're my true wingman. To my unborn nephew, I can't wait to hold you in my arms. For Joan, liberté, egalité, fraternité! To Beth, Donnie, and Iris*—*my heart. To Wyndie, Julie, and Lynne, creative wunderkinds and my Anti-Bride girlfriends. To Dave and Erin, Don and Jenny, and Niall and Jeannie*—*my tribe. To Nick and Elise Lowe. To Mikyla Bruder, the girl who turned fantasy into reality. To Kerry Colburn, Michele Posner, and Amy Ennis for your style and know-how. To Ithinand Tubkam, my creative soul mate. To Michaela for your nonstop genius and being in my corner, and Amy Glynn Hornick. To Michael for your wisdom and love. To my adored French family, the Gerins*—*je vous aime!*

Kathleen Hughes *For Nick; thank you for the best seven years of my life; I look forward to our new addition; for my father and late mother, for being in my corner no matter what choices I made in life; for Liz, Jules, Tina, Lizzette, and Deena*—*the best friends a person could have. For Katy, for showing me what this town is made of; for Dori, thanks for being my sounding board and a good friend; for my sisters, Joan and Carolyn, two excellent role models and true Anti-Brides.*

Amy Glynn Hornick *For my girlfriends*—*especially Jennifer Moulton*—*for their ideas, experiences, humor, and advice. To Patrick, for your soothing voice and late-night chats. To Anne for strength, silliness, and encouragement. For Sarah (the dog) for always knowing how I felt. To Kathy for all of your hard work, persistence, and easygoing nature. Finally, a big thanks to Carolyn for dreaming up Anti-Bride and offering to share her with me.*

Special thanks to the talented, kind, and generous people who offered their time and energy to make this book a reality:

Kara Adamson, L'Auberge Soleil; Beth Blake and Sophie Simmons, Thread Design; Michaela Brockstedt, Target; Bridget Brown, Bella Bridesmaid; Nick Brown Photography; Bradley Burch; Karen Chesshire, Sima's Cakes; Donna Davis, Forbeadin'; A Day in May; Peg Devlin, Peg Devlin Catering; photographer Karina Marie Diaz; Kay Dillion, Beauxgateaux Cakes; Emily Dolan and Susan Morgan, Elegant Cheesecakes; hairstylist James Dunham; the DuWop girls, Cristina Bartolucci and Laura Deluisa; floral designer and wedding planner Jolie Fay; Janis Fein, Sea Ranch Lodge; Amy Goodman, In Style; Lisa Holt, Milliken Creek; Sonja Hong, Butterfly Cakes; makeup genius Jane Iredale; Catherine Kitz and Grace Street Catering; David Leven and Russ Catanach for help in the music section; Kellie Little, Zindagi Salon; Jeanine Lobel, Stila; Lisa Mackey Jewelry; Carol Marino, A Perfect Wedding; Elizabeth Mayhew, Real Simple; Niall McCallum, Empson USA; singer-songwriter/musician Natasha Miller; Fran Myers, Your Special Day; Jean Picard, Jean Picard Wedding Consulting; skin gurus Dr. Vail Reese and Shari Spakes; Litsa Rorris, Wedding Bells; She She Events; Taste Catering; Joyce C. Smith, Weddings Unlimited, Inc.; Crys Stewart, Wedding Bells; Larissa Thompson, In Style; and for every bride past and present who had the guts to challenge the Wedding Industrial Complex.

For news and updates, check out **www.antibride.com**.

Chapter 1

Getting Started: Fantasy to Reality
{Gearing up for the long haul}

WHY YOU BOUGHT THIS BOOK & HOW IT CAN HELP YOU

A film reel of your wedding has probably been playing in your head ever since you dressed up Barbie and Ken and walked them down the aisle. Now's your chance to star in your own production, whether that means arriving in a blue limo or riding Harleys to the top of a mountain to exchange "I dos." Any wedding, large or small, simple or complex, involves more details, foresight, and multitasking than most events you will ever produce in your lifetime, but you need not go it alone! Introducing your new best friend: the *Anti-Bride Wedding Planner*, designed to give you the most essentially edited, yet quint-essentially erudite, information in an easy-to-use format. If you are looking for boring perfection, you won't find it here. Great ideas culled from creative people, as well as helpful forms and thought-provoking tips and tricks, will help give you the Zen you'll need to get to the finish line in style.

What makes the *Anti-Bride Wedding Planner* different from other wedding planners? Most wedding planners are like telephone books; they're so elegant and oversized that most brides end up never using them. *Enough!*

The Anti-Bride philosophy is simple: It's all about **you**. The days of bowing to the preconceived notion of what society expects of a bride (or a wedding) are over. We can imagine nothing more excruciating than turning six months (or more) of your life into a series of endless lists, errands, and spreadsheets— all for the end result of transforming yourself into a white tulle–embellished, cookie-cutter version of every other bride out there. The Anti-Bride philosophy celebrates individuality, personal style, and taste. It encourages independent thinking and applauds creativity with a dash of thriftiness. We want to help you design an event that reflects who you really are. And, most of all, we want you to enjoy the journey and adventure of a lifetime!

The *Anti-Bride Wedding Planner* is designed for mobility. It can fit in a tote bag, and it can weather abuse— from cake frosting to makeup smudges to martini mishaps. It's packed with useful tips and tricks that will help you brainstorm the possibilities in a way that the other wedding tomes won't. We've also included questionnaires (to help you find vendors), pockets (for all those pictures, swatches, and business cards you collect along the way), and white space (for your notes and doodles).

Instructions for a Successful Planning Effort (and Subsequent Life)

❋ Take this planner everywhere you go! Your best ideas and inspirations may come to you in surprising places.

❋ Flexibility, a realistic budget, and research can be your best friends, so keep an open mind.

❋ Pay attention—the devil's in the details.

❋ Be a genius—borrow from others instead of reinventing the wheel.

❋ Be bold, but never be bossy. No one likes a Bridezilla!

❋ Exercise your sense of humor (and body) often. Happy, glowing people live longer.

❋ Have sex—and have it often.

❋ Make time for date nights. Your wedding will last a day, but your marriage will last a lot longer.

❋ Drink gallons of water, watch the booze, and sleep deeply.

❋ **Anti-Bride Tip** | *A Saturday night in spring or summer is most popular with brides. Consider a Friday night or Sunday afternoon instead—the price difference will **surprise you.***

Your Budget

The reality of knot tying is that bliss can fizzle out like day-old champagne once the planning begins. But Anti-Brides can still have the soirée of the decade without nose-diving into a financial folly—the key is deciding what's most important, setting a budget, and sticking to it. You may not be able to afford the W Hotel, but perhaps the local museum has a room available that's twice as nice. Be open to different avenues, and your bank account will love you for it. Think back to other weddings. Don't they all kind of blur together? The ones we remember are the ones at which money wasn't the focus and creativity reigned: the wedding in the rustic barn with homemade treats from the neighbors and the rockabilly band; the one with an uncle's handcrafted microbrew; the one with the late-afternoon sun shining through the trees. Many things in the world don't have price tags but are more beautiful than anything money could ever buy. Look for the meaning in your wedding, and you'll find your message.

❋ **Anti-Bride Tip** | *Allocate your money wisely. The biggest mistake brides make is spending the bulk of the cash in the beginning. Wedding pro Carol Marino says, "The bride and groom will book an expensive room right away and then realize it leaves little money for anything else."*

So, first things first. How much can you afford to spend? Once you know your budget, you'll need to be prepared to make tough choices regarding how you want to allocate your resources. Most important, your (yours and your partner's) vision and priorities are what matter. If you're focused, realistic, and creative, you can have the perfect wedding within any budget.

❋ **Anti-Bride Tip|** *Buyer, beware! Put all deposits on a credit card. Transactions are easier to track. You'll also be protected under federal consumer protection laws and the buyer protection service offered by the card company. If the vendor drops the ball, you contest the charges.*

❋ **Anti-Bride Tip|** *Share your budget and collection of magazine photos when you interview potential vendors to get them closer to your headspace. They can often dream up something special to match your vision and price range.*

❋ **Anti-Bride Tip|** *Start a bidding war, and name your price! Seek estimates from at least five vendors in major categories such as photography, flowers, attire, reception site, and caterers, and record their bids.*

Setting the Stage

Before you begin, use the space below to describe the elements of your dream wedding. If you've been to other weddings, there may be a particular detail, location, tradition, and creative approach that you love. Before you start planning, get your thoughts down on paper—you'll be surprised how a simple stream-of-consciousness list of ideas can help you set priorities before you're officially buried in wedding details.

✳Skimp

INVITATIONS

Order online because cost savings are significant. Look for complete packages—from invitations to a wedding Web site.

CALLIGRAPHER

Hire art students from a local college to address invitations and announcements. They need the money; you need the quality for less.

FLOWERS

Buy in-season flowers and only what you need. Allocate the bulk of the arrangements to the reception where guests spend the most time. If you plan far enough in advance, you can even harvest your own flowers.

MEAL CHOICES

Choosing dishes like chicken, beef, salmon, and shrimp, and steering clear of pricier items like filet mignon, can save you a lot. Meals for a daytime wedding also cost considerably less than those for an evening one.

DRESS

Beautiful alternatives are available in local boutiques or your favorite department store's eveningwear section. Some Web sites, like *Indiebride.com*, sponsor a dress swap.

ACCESSORIES

Vintage accessories can be funked up if you know the gal in the bead shop. Donna Davis of Forbeadin' takes apart Grandma's classics and adds glamour with semiprecious stones. She also makes tiaras that convert into necklaces after the event.

✳Spend

PHOTOGRAPHER

Rely on recommendations from friends, relatives, and pros you know. View their portfolios online, and hire the photographer with the best one.

WEDDING CONSULTANT

For large weddings, a good one can be a godsend. As your girl Friday, she will be able to take on the lion's share of the wedding stress. *(Note: Weddings are her industry; expect industry discounts.)*

CAKE

Unless you or your best friend is a pastry chef, don't attempt to make your own wedding cake to cut costs.

FOOD QUALITY

Good food can mean the difference between an unforgettable evening and grumpy guests. Too often, caterers underestimate portions. Choose chicken over prime rib, but never skimp on the quality (or quantity) of your ingredients.

BOOZE

The approach is pizzazz without a huge bar bill, but running out of liquor is a no-no. Good beer, good wine, and a snappy cocktail are all you need. Negotiate case discounts with a vineyard, shop at a regional discount shop (such as Trader Joe's), or check out the wine picks of Target's new sommelier.

LABOR

Experienced people will keep your guests happy. Make sure they're pros.

Timeline Checklist

Whether you're planning the big day in a one-year time frame or in two weeks, there's a method to the madness. Obviously, the things you have to book—rooms, bands, honeymoon suites, and catering—need to be considered before anything else. If you only have a month or two to prepare, you may only have a matter of days to take care of each stage of the process.

1. FIRST THINGS FIRST: THE BASICS

- ✗ Set up a filing system. (Accordion files are great for this!)
- ✗ Choose the time of year.
- ✗ Decide on a wedding and a honeymoon budget.
- ✗ Decide on your priorities—food and band? Venue and cake? Libations and dress? Number of guests? Then allocate your budget accordingly.
- ✗ Start looking at venues and ceremony locations based on the ballpark budget; see if they're available when you need them. Make sure the date does not conflict with any major religious holidays—not just your own!
- ✗ Start gathering honeymoon information. Begin a dialogue with a travel agent to make things easier.
- ✗ Choose bridal and groom attendants. Run the idea by them to see if they're up to the job.

Notes:

2. SELECT VENDORS

- ✗ Hire an officiant.
- ☐ Hire a wedding consultant/planner, if needed.
- ✗ Interview and hire photographer/videographer, florist, cake baker, and caterer.
- ✗ Decide on the type of music desired for the ceremony and reception. Interview and hire a band or DJ. If you're doing your own music, start compiling now.
- ✗ Research and book limousine or vintage car rentals or other transportation.
- ✗ Look at invitations. Nail down a style that you like, and narrow down different typefaces, paper stock, etc.
- ✗ Decide where to register. Start choosing desired items; add them to your list.

Notes:

3. CHOOSE ATTIRE AND COLOR SCHEME

- ☒ Determine your wedding colors and think about decorations.
- ☒ Choose and order your wedding dress and veil.
- ☐ Buy undergarments for the wedding attire. (You need them prior to fittings.)
- ☒ Look for bridesmaids' dresses.
- ☒ Pick out tuxedos or suits for attendants.
- ☒ Buy the rings.
- ☒ Choose and order invitations.

Notes:

4. PRE-PARTIES AND CEREMONY STUFF

- ☐ Begin writing the vows, and choose readings or prose for the ceremony.
- ☐ Choose ceremony, reception, and rehearsal dinner music.
- ☒ Choose and book the desired location for the rehearsal dinner.
- ☐ Look for and block rooms at a nearby hotel for out-of-town guests.
- ☐ Decide if programs or personalized napkins will be purchased, and order them.
- ☒ Make a final list of invites, and compile addresses. Use the Who's Invited Worksheet later in this chapter.
- ☐ Send out save-the-date cards.

Notes:

5. ADMINISTRATIVE DETAILS

- ☐ Get directions to the ceremony site, from the site to the reception, and from the site to the rehearsal dinner.
- ☐ Make a short list of things to do in the wedding town to include with the directions, if applicable.
- ☐ Check your passports and visas if you're honeymooning outside the country.
- ☐ Buy or make reception favors.
- ☐ Nail down flower arrangements with florist; if centerpieces are not floral, coordinate with friends and vendors.
- ☐ Choose the reception food; confirm with the caterer.
- ☒ Address (or have a friend or relative address) wedding invitations. Send them out at least six weeks in advance.
- ☐ Reserve accommodations and transportation for out-of-town guests. Send out a newsletter or correspondence to update them on the wedding itinerary and important names and numbers.
- ☐ Schedule manicure, pedicure, hair, brows, dermatologist, and spa appointments for the day before the wedding. Make sure to give yourself a few months to experiment with your hair and makeup.
- ☐ Arrange for alterations.
- ☐ Get a marriage license.

Notes:

6. LAST-MINUTE DETAILS

- ☐ Call guests who have not responded to invitations.
- ☐ Confirm the time and date of wedding rehearsal with the wedding party. Make sure they have everything they need.
- ☐ ~~Stop mail and newspapers while you are away on your honeymoon, or get someone to pick it up for you.~~
- ☐ ~~Get tickets and itinerary for your trip.~~
- ☐ ~~Make a list of honeymoon location emergency numbers and credit card numbers and make copies of passports to leave at home with both sets of parents or dependable friends.~~
- ☐ Try on your wedding gown to check fit. Make sure it's pressed.
- ☐ Make up an emergency kit with essentials to have on hand for wedding and reception. (See Chapter 5.)
- ☐ Buy a gift for your sweetie.
- ☐ Finalize the wedding program.
- ☐ Have the bachelorette party.

Notes:

_____

_____

7. DOWN-TO-THE-WIRE STUFF

- ☐ Run through the details with all vendors.
- ☐ Confirm rehearsal and wedding plans with attendants.
- ☐ Put together all of the elements of your outfit.
- ☐ Finish packing for the honeymoon.
- ☐ Get a massage or go to yoga.

Notes:

_____

_____

8. DAY BEFORE

- ☐ Head for the salon: Get a manicure and pedicure, and your hair done.
- ☐ Get (and pack!) the cake knife.
- ☐ Give your sweetie the present.

Notes:

_____

_____

9. BIG DAY

- ☐ Do your hair and makeup.
- ☐ Eat a cheeseburger about an hour and a half before you're ready to take off (the protein and fat will see you through until the sit-down dinner); eat a garden burger with cheese if you're a veggie.
- ☐ Have ONE glass of champagne to calm your nerves before you hit the red carpet.
- ☐ Relax.
- ☐ Get married!

Wedding Style Worksheet

Use this worksheet to brainstorm your ideas and thoughts.

SEASON/MONTH

First Choice: Fall / October

Second Choice:

Third Choice:

Notes:

TIME OF DAY

☐ Morning ☒ Afternoon ☒ Evening ☐ Other

WEDDING THEME IDEAS

First Choice: Maple leaves

Second Choice:

Third Choice:

Notes:

DESIRED NUMBER OF GUESTS 115-120

TYPE OF RECEPTION

☐ Cocktail ☐ Champagne Brunch ☐ Luncheon

☒ Buffet Dinner ☐ Weekend Wedding ☐ Sit-Down Dinner

RECEPTION LOCATION

First Choice: Wysocki's Lake Park Manor

Second Choice:

Third Choice:

Notes:

Setting Priorities

Part of fine-tuning your wedding day is figuring out your priorities. What's most important to you? Are you a lounge lizard who loves to dance the night away to a jazz combo? Do you fantasize about Jamie Oliver's culinary wizardry? Is a hair-raising pre-wedding adventure with your pals or a heart-stopping view nonnegotiable? Every Anti-Bride wants it all. But until money starts growing on trees, you need to start making some decisions. This doesn't mean that reality can't match up to fantasy. The following questions can help you figure out where to pony up the dollars and where to fake it:

1. WHEN I THINK OF PUTTING ON MY GROOVE, I THINK OF:
A) a Latin salsa band
B) a string quartet
C) Tommy Dorsey and Glenn Miller (big band)
D) a little something for everyone (Grandma and my indie-rock friends)

2. MY FAVORITE THING TO DO IS:
A) go for a long hike or bike ride
B) put on my sexiest clubbing gear, and dance until sunrise
C) host a dinner party
D) plan my next weekend getaway

3. I WANT MY WEDDING DRESS TO BE: *None*
A) a beautiful, simple sundress
B) a custom-made gown with beads and antique lace
C) a scuba suit
D) a foxy vintage gown

4. FOOD IS:
A) the nectar of the gods
B) like bread—it nourishes and satisfies (read: American diner)
C) an energy bar between meetings
D) best when cooked by someone else

5. MY FAVORITE DINNER IS:
A) a filet mignon with saffron risotto and   *None*
   asparagus vinaigrette
B) a burrito and a beer
C) anything barbecued
D) something from the "gourmet" freezer section

6. MY IDEAL CELEBRATION WOULD BE:
A) a candlelit soirée in Provence with close friends
B) an intimate fireside dinner for two
C) a backpacking excursion through the Himalayas
D) a beach barbecue at sundown

7. EVERY YEAR, I LOOK FORWARD TO:
A) the leaves changing with the seasons
B) snowball fights and snowboarding
C) spring breezes and green countryside
D) swimming, surfing, and beach parties

8. MY FRIENDS WOULD DESCRIBE ME AS:
A) a party animal
B) Susie Socialite
C) a fringe dweller (an aficionado of foreign films and everything underground)
D) easily overwhelmed

9. FAMILY WILL BE INVOLVED IN PLANNING:
A) nothing—my friends know me best
B) everything! They owe me after my sister's wedding
C) 50-50: I'll let his mom and my mom duke it out
D) as much as they want; this will be a beautiful family-bonding experience

OTHER THINGS TO ASK YOURSELF:

❋ Toasts: Do I want people to bare all, or shut up and eat?

Shut up & eat

❋ Bridesmaids: Do I want my own personal entourage, or to sidestep the dress selection and fitting production altogether?

Personal entourage

❋ Vows: Do I want a very consecrated atmosphere that includes quotes from the Bible/Torah/Koran/I Ching, or no mention of anything resembling organized religion?

Sumewhat religious, traditional

❋ His outfit: Can he walk in shoes other than Doc Martens? Does he want me to shop with him so that our outfits coordinate? Am I okay with a surprise getup?

Shop with him

❋ Walking down the aisle: Is there an aisle? Am I okay with "Here Comes the Bride," or do I want something more personal? How can I include my six parents so that they all feel important?

Here comes the bride

Expense Worksheet

Every wedding is different—an at-home wedding may cost significantly less than a wedding at a local winery, but on average, the cost of a wedding these days is around $20,000. Typically, most of the money is spent on the reception (including catering), rings, and attire. At this point, pencil in rough numbers based on your general budget. Come back to this list as things become more firm.

ITEM	PROJECTED COST	ACTUAL COST	DEPOSIT	BALANCE DUE
Attire (Bride)		$753.84	$376.00	$377.84
Attire (Groom)		$0.00	$0.00	$0.00
Invitations		$180.25	—	
Reception/Catering			$500	
Transportation		$799.00	$200.00	$599.00
Ceremony		$500	$100	$400
Officiant				
Rings/Jewelry				
Cake				
Music		$495.00	$100.00	$395.00
Photography/Videography		$850	$300	$550
Flowers				
Miscellaneous				

✳Questions for the Event Planner

Have this list of questions handy when visiting planners—or keep it by the phone for quick reference.

1. HOW LONG HAVE YOU BEEN IN THE BUSINESS? HOW MANY WEDDINGS HAVE YOU PLANNED?
   (Don't discount someone new to the business if you get a good vibe from her otherwise. Chances are someone new to the industry will tend to overdeliver and undercharge, thus landing you a really great deal!)

2. WHAT CAN YOU DO FOR ME TO HELP ME PLAN MY WEDDING?
   (Each planner has a different style and skill set. Do you want help to plan the entire event from the beginning? Or do you just need referrals and help pulling it all together at the end? Do you want help coming up with creative touches to make your wedding unique? Make sure you are clear on your needs.)

3. CAN I SEE SOME PHOTOS OF YOUR WORK? WHAT IS YOUR STYLE AND APPROACH?
   (While the planner's work is mostly behind the scenes, seeing photos of weddings that she is proud of will give you a sense of her aesthetic and the vendors she works with.)

4. HOW MANY WEDDINGS DO YOU DO ON A WEEKEND? IN A MONTH?
   (Knowing this will give you an idea of the kind of attention you will receive.)

5. HOW WILL MY WEDDING BE STAFFED? HOW WILL YOU STAFF MY WEDDING IF SOMETHING COMES UP AND YOU CAN'T BE THERE?
   (Even a simple wedding benefits from having at least two event planning staff on duty. Often, event planners are sole proprietors. Make sure there is a backup plan.)

6. WHAT WAS A STICKY SITUATION THAT YOU HAD TO RESOLVE QUICKLY TO SAVE THE DAY IN A PAST WEDDING? CAN YOU DESCRIBE A MOMENT THAT YOU ARE PROUDEST OF? WHAT WAS YOUR FAVORITE WEDDING, AND WHY?

7. ARE YOU COMFORTABLE USING THE INTERNET? DO YOU HAVE AN E-MAIL ADDRESS?
   (Chances are you are addicted to these means of communication. You will want to pick a planner that is, too.)

Who's Invited

The guest list always seems to be a stumbling block in the planning process—parents don't want to offend that aunt you see only at funerals and weddings, so they try to strong-arm you into "just one more." No! Set your rules, and be firm. It's best to establish your criteria and explain it to your parents, future in-laws, and others before any planning even begins. Set your number and fill in the blanks. No exceptions. With established rules in place, the process will go that much smoother.

Use the sheet below to set up your criteria. For example, some couples use the "every guest needs to know both of us" rule. From there, establish your "A," "B," and "C" lists. The "A" list should contain names of people who must be there; the "B" list, names of people who should be there; and the "C" list, the names of those whom you'd like to be there if there's room.

Criteria for Choosing Guests:

1. _____

2. _____

3. _____

4. _____

CAROLYN AND LAURENT GERIN'S GUEST LIST STRATEGY

Carolyn and Laurent had three receptions to keep things streamlined. The San Francisco party had only those people in their life every week, who had helped them move, or were a part of their chosen tribe. Once they started editing with this criteria, it became easy. The Washingtion, DC, party was immediate family, Carolyn's college friends, close neighbors, and her parents' friends. Because it was at home, there was a natural size restriction. The Paris party was immediate family only.

Who's Invited

A List

_____

_____

_____

_____

*

B List

_____

_____

_____

_____

_____

_____

_____

_____

_____

_____

_____

_____

_____

_____

_____

_____

C List

_____

_____

_____

_____

_____

_____

_____

_____

_____

_____

_____

_____

_____

_____

_____

_____

Final Guest List

Name	Address	Telephone	RSVP Received?	Number Coming
Richard & Shirley Andreas				
Kara Annable & guest				
Robert & Jenifer Bettinelli				
Donald & Carmalee Blok				
Todd & Susan Cain				
Sarah Cleveland & guest				
Curtis & Nancy Cole				
Russell Cornish				
Tifanie Coyne				
Elisa Cregg				
Jessica Cregg				
Mark & Sandy Cregg				
Shawn Cregg				
Mildred Crispell				
Patrick Ochsner & Emilee Dupe				
Colin Duncan				
Gary Duncan & guest				
Maggie Duncan				
Summer Duncan				
Kenneth & Kelly Edgar				
Nicole Esposito				
Jerry Farnett & guest				
Helen Farrell & Otto Church				
Martin & Sharon Gendron				
John & Donna Giarrusso				

Final Guest List

Name	Address	Telephone	RSVP Received?	Number Coming
Bill & Jessica Glod				
Edward Greean				
Edward & Kristen Greean				
Irine Greean				
Frank & Ernestine Guzur				
Richard & Rebecca Guzur				
Allen Hatch				
Kevin & Amy Hatch				
David Hatch & guest				
Donald & Martha Hatch				
James & Jennifer Hatch				
Karen Hatch & Rachel Miller				
Paul & Sharon Helfeld				
June Hile				
Patrick & Carolyn Holmes				
Bradley & Theresa Hunold				
James Johnson & guest				
Michael & Joanne Kane				
Sally Kwasigroch				
Thomas Knasigroch & Christine Newell				
Robin Launt				
Corey & Jennifer Leible				
Brittany Leonard & Mitchell Pallone				
Emily Leonard				
Amanda Lord				
Sherry Lord				

Final Guest List

Name	Address	Telephone	RSVP Received?	Number Coming
Chris & Michele Maestri				
Daniel Marshall				
Megan Maycumber & guest				
Justin & Elizabeth Meyers				
Bill & Sharon Monte				
Gene & Louise Mooney				
Todd & Brenda Mulhern				
Mark Ochsner & Kiersten Park				
Michael & Vicki Ochsner				
Ryan Ochsner				
Doreen & Timothy Palmer				
Brian Patrick & guest				
Michael Patrick & guest				
James & Brenda Perrotti				
Allen & Anna Perry				
Edward & Cheryl Pochatko				
Jeremy & Christina Pochatko				
Joseph Prince				
Kara Prince & guest				
Steven & Renee Quinn				
Ronnie Reusswig & Jamie Stevens				
Todd & Megan Rheaume				
Chris & Cindy Sarazin				
George & Ann Signor				
Casey Simek & guest				
Joseph & Anna Simek				

Final Guest List

Name	Address	Telephone	RSVP Received?	Number Coming
Brent & Christina Smith				
David & Darlene Stevens				
Dylan Stevens				
James Sullivan				
Brian Tonks				
Francie Tonks				
Margaret Wieczorek				
Thomas & Margaret Wieczorek				
Luther & Kathleen Wiers				
James & Sheila Wilson				
Christiana Young				
Curtis & Lori Young				
Joshua & Jessica Young				
Allen & Katie Perry				
Taylor & Alex Perry				

Notes

Notes

❋ **Anti-Bride Tip** | *Says Elizabeth Mayhew, the style editor of* Real Simple *magazine, begin by setting a budget, getting organized, and delegating as much as possible. You need all the help you can get, so start asking. "Your mother-in-law and your mother are perfect candidates. Then, move on to your bridesmaids (if you have them)—part of their job is to help you. Most people will want to lend a hand, and if they don't, the worst thing they can say is 'no, thank you.'"*

Notes

Notes

Chapter 2

Offbeat Spaces & Plans for Places
{Brainstorming for your wedding wheres}

A wedding can happen anywhere—from a rustic barn to a ski lodge in summertime. While common spaces, like hotels, offer perks such as room discounts, they may also coerce you into choosing polyester tablecloths, frozen hors d'oeuvres, or worse, the dreaded ice sculpture.

Finding the "space less married in," however, requires some extra footwork and even some cajoling. A farmer might not think his abandoned barn a dreamy site, but with the right ideas and negotiations, it could be yours. An ocean view might have a big price tag at a seaside B&B, but the seafood restaurant or the Elks Club down the road might be ideal.

The biggest challenge is information overload—you'll need to set up a system to keep track of details. The right wedding venue may appear entirely by accident. Get in the car with a map, some sandwiches, and your sweetie, and go on a day trip—you never know what undiscovered gems you may find!

As you finalize your choices for space, fill in The Phone Book at the back of the planner for a handy all-in-one info location.

Costumed Camaraderie

T. A. and Jasper were married at dusk beneath redwoods by an Internet minister dressed as Joey Ramone. She wore a medieval gown; Jasper dressed as Napoleon. Guests made or rented costumes in lieu of bringing gifts. A flower-savvy friend designed her bouquet and centerpieces using black roses, coffee beans, broccoli, and other vegetables. An "econo-bar"—a self-serve table with buckets of ice-cold beer and cases of wine— was set up. Creative thinking like this can turn even a modest event into something extraordinary.

THE CEREMONY

The moment of truth—that defining point where you pledge your love to one another in front of those closest to you. The sky's the limit on how you want this message translated. There are, however, some practicalities to consider first. For instance, do you want a religious or civil ceremony?

If you decide on a religious ceremony, you may be required to undergo premarital counseling or become a church member. If you're part of an interfaith or same-sex couple, don't wait until the last minute to book the only rabbi or Buddhist monk in your area who will officiate a "mixed" marriage or a same-sex commitment ceremony. Civil ceremonies don't have as much cultural overhead as religious ceremonies and can be as simple as standing in front of a judge and saying "I do."

Whichever ceremony you choose, your setting options are endless. Offbeat settings offer more flexibility than churches or synagogues, where protocols may need to be adhered to. Hold the wedding ceremony at the reception site and do away with many complications.

❈ **Anti-Bride Tip** | *Check out chambers of commerce, city halls, and visitors bureaus for space ideas. Other alternative spaces to check out include officer's clubs, local orchards or wineries, union or VFW halls, off-season ski resorts, amusement parks, movie studio lots, school and university grounds, or even historic boats.*

THINGS TO CONSIDER WHEN CHOOSING A SPACE

❈ *Size Does Matter:* Get a ballpark idea of who's invited and round out that number to help target your search for the perfect space. Remember, the space may look roomy now but it will fill up fast with a band setup, buffet, tables, chairs, and decorations.

❈ *Hell Is Other People:* If you want something intimate, don't hold your event in a public spot like a park or garden unless you rent it. Strangers may walk by, look, or even make comments.

❈ *If These Walls Could Talk:* Big venues often hold more than one event at a time, so find out what's happening on your target date, and where. You don't want to be shouting your vows over the sounds of karaoke or a self-help seminar next door.

❈ *Room with a View:* Give your guests a little feast for their eyes. Pick a location that offers some thing visual—a city skyline or a sunset overlooking the ocean. If you choose a historic building or museum, look at the architectural details, wall hangings, and floor coverings.

❈ *Praying to the Parking Gods:* If you are having a city wedding, look for a lot nearby and negotiate a flat rate to validate your guests' passes. Opting for a bus or trolley may be a solution for inadequate parking facilities.

RECEPTION SPACES: PROS & CONS

If you can rent it, you can probably have your wedding there. Here's a guide to some common and not-so-common spaces.

Space	Pros	Cons
Home Sweet Home	Meaningful, informal, flexible, familiar, and best of all, private. With friends and family pitching in, labor costs less.	Rental overload, noise ordinances, limited space, storage and insurance costs, inadequate outlets and PARKING.
Catering Hall/Hotel	One-stop shopping: rentals, a full-service staff, catering, a banquet room, room discounts for you and your guests.	One-stop shopping comes with a hefty price tag. Rigid schedules and menus, production-line food, extra charges for valet parking, corkage fee, cake cutting.
Bar/Restaurant	Space issues—use it to explain why you couldn't invite the office. A low-cost option. If you're a regular, or you met your sweetie there, it's meaningful.	Space issues—can everyone you want to invite fit? Inadequate facilities and parking. Bars may not have a kitchen.
Private Club (such as a country or social club)	No wedding-factory feel. Fewer people to deal with and better service. Beautiful sites and sceneries, such as golf courses or skyline views.	May need to be a member or be sponsored. Expensive. Commissioned caterers and varying food quality.
Civic Site (historic and university buildings, park, garden, museum)	Subsidized by taxpayers, these can be a great bargain. Parks and gardens are natural, beautiful backdrops, so fewer flowers are needed.	Often have time and beverage restrictions. Keep in the mind that setup may have to take place after closing (4 or 5 P.M.).
Exotic Destination	Intimate—a great excuse for a limited guest list. A beautiful, unusual setting and a potential vacation experience.	Expensive, but remember, you're not feeding 150 guests. Possible language and cultural barriers.

31

IDEAS FROM SHE SHE EVENT DESIGN

❋ Couples often don't know what to do about children at a wedding. Set up a play area in a corner of the reception and staff it with two nannies. Have a special kids' table topped with goody bags filled with treats.

❋ One couple recently completed a backpacking trip to Europe. They named each table after a city they had visited and cleverly displayed a photo and a diary entry as part of the table's centerpiece.

❋ A couple created a wedding crossword puzzle that tests the guests' knowledge of them and placed a copy at each place setting. The tables were named after the various answers to the clues.

❋ Another couple made donations to various charities in lieu of favors. Included in each guest's escort card was a note of donation to a charity made in that guest's name. The couple tried to match the charity chosen for each guest to issues close to the guest's heart.

A Luau Wedding by She She Event Design

One offbeat couple chose a luau-themed wedding. The groom set the tone by changing post-ceremony into a Hawaiian shirt, shorts, and sandals, and his groomsmen followed suit. There was a luau-inspired menu and tropical floral arrangements, with dining tables named after islands. Steel drums played during the cocktail hour. After dinner, a band played reggae classics into the night.

❋**Anti-Bride Tip** | *Obtain a contract with the agreed-upon costs from all vendors. Keep copies in a binder. Assign someone to bring the binder to your event in case any issues arise.*

FRIENDS & FAMILY

Brent and Tricia are crafty, thrifty, and smart. They negotiated a daytime Saturday wedding at a hip restaurant in San Francisco close to their home. The restaurant projected vintage Italian films onto the side of a large building in the courtyard, while heat lamps kept guests toasty. Heavy hors d'oeuvres circulated before a buffet-style feast of French country fare was served. Mojitos and margaritas were served along with Napa Valley varietals. After the event, close friends of the couple grabbed the flower arrangements and traveled six blocks by cab to 26-Mix, a cocktail lounge, where they threw an unforgettable after-party for the couple. Inside, guests were greeted with magical red velvet–quilted walls, hushed lighting, ambient music, and pendant lamps of orange and red. For embellishment, roses from the wedding were tied to beer taps using ribbon. Centerpieces were Chinese fans, firecrackers, chopsticks, confetti, and lit candles. The lounge owners printed up special "wedding currency" drink tickets and offered up an open bar, an amazing DJ, and the gorgeous centerpieces. The celebration of good friendships (and great cocktails!) and the new bride and groom went well into the evening with '80s new-wave hits and lots of dancing.

Transportation: When the Rubber Hits the Road

One detail many leave to the last minute is transportation. Although you're not expected to pick up the tab for rental cars for the weekend, try to make it hassle-free for your attendants. Recruit friends, set up car pools, negotiate discounts with cab or bus companies, but don't belabor the point.

Decide on wedding wheels early, especially if you want that Gatsby stretch limo. Don't rule out alternatives like a 1950s road boat, a horse-drawn carriage, a Harley, or a 1960s Astin Martin. Local car clubs have the skinny on how to get a photo-fabulous set of wheels for less than you think it costs. Yeah, baby!

LIMOUSINES: *There is a reason why rock stars favor limos—they are elegant and non-egalitarian, and entrances are guaranteed to be dramatic. While limos have plenty of amenities, such as plush carpeting, champagne, and maybe even a TV or sunroof, they run about $60 per hour with a minimum rental time. However, the last thing an Anti-Bride would do on the way to her ceremony is watch CNN. The champagne (if it's good), well, that's another story! To save on costs, try a car from a funeral home. Yup, usually, you can get it for more than half the cost of a traditional limo service. Just take the white curtains out of the windows. Or leave 'em in, and run all the red lights!*

LUXURY CAR: *Groove cruise. Many car-rental companies rent Caddies and Lincolns for as little as $50 per day. You'll need to find a driver (like a friend or relative), but the cost-saving is worth it.*

TROLLEY OR BUS: *Trolley-ho! Some cities rent trolleys that accommodate 30 people or more. You probably don't want to arrive at the chapel in a two-ton bus yourself, but it's a nice option if you have several out-of-town guests or don't want to deal with traffic congestion between the ceremony and the reception. This is also a great way to avoid any drunk-driving complications.*

HORSE-DRAWN BUGGY: *A horse-drawn buggy is a romantic way to make your big entrance and something you'll always remember. There are limitations and costs for this luxury. Count on your ride being about $80 per hour, and plan on getting yourself to a designated pickup spot.*

Ceremony Site Worksheet

Site #1

Location: Dewitt Comm. Ch. Contact: Carlie Watson

Phone: (315)445-0331 Fax: (315)445-2769

E-mail: office @ (url) URL: dewittchurch.org

Number of Guests Site Can Accommodate: 700

Deposit Required: $100.00 Cancellation Policy: non-refundable

Special Restrictions: None - unity candle, pew bows and center piece use free.

Site #2

Location: _____ Contact: _____

Phone: _____ Fax: _____

E-mail: _____ URL: _____

Number of Guests Site Can Accommodate: _____

Deposit Required: _____ Cancellation Policy: _____

Special Restrictions: _____

Site #3

Location: _____ Contact: _____

Phone: _____ Fax: _____

E-mail: _____ URL: _____

Number of Guests Site Can Accommodate: _____

Deposit Required: _____ Cancellation Policy: _____

Special Restrictions: _____

Reception Site Worksheet

Site #1

Location: Wysocki's   Contact: Ann/Jimmy

Phone: 315-699-7828   Fax:

E-mail: URL: wysockis.com

Number of Guests Site Can Accommodate: 225

Deposit Required: $500.00   Cancellation Policy: 1/2 refund if re-

Special Restrictions: no credit cards-cash/ck   booked

On-Site Catering? (Y)/N   If yes, notes regarding menu and cost: $11.75 - $12.25/person

Included: ☑Tables ☑Linens ☑Dinnerware ☑Chairs ☑Kitchen facilities

Beverages Available: Yes   Corkage Fee: $50.00 bar-
tender

Cake Baking? Y/(N)   If yes, notes regarding styles available:

Cake Cutting? Y/(N)   If yes, cake-cutting fee: No

Music:

Is there enough power to handle a band/DJ? (Y)/N   Is there a dance floor? (Y)/N

Deposit Required: Cancellation Policy:

Special Restrictions:

❋Notes:

Linen napkins for head table, immediate family, ¢35 for each additional guest, paper napkins free. Brown, silver, watermelon not available.

Site #2

Location: _____ Contact: _____

Phone: _____ Fax: _____

E-mail: _____ URL: _____

Number of Guests Site Can Accommodate: _____

Deposit Required: _____ Cancellation Policy: _____

Special Restrictions: _____

On-Site Catering? Y/N If yes, notes regarding menu and cost: _____

Included: ☐ Tables ☐ Linens ☐ Dinnerware ☐ Chairs ☐ Kitchen facilities

Beverages Available: _____ Corkage Fee: _____

Cake Baking? Y/N If yes, notes regarding styles available: _____

Cake Cutting? Y/N If yes, cake-cutting fee: _____

Music: _____

Is there enough power to handle a band/DJ? Y/N Is there a dance floor? Y/N

Deposit Required: _____ Cancellation Policy: _____

Special Restrictions: _____

❋Notes:

_____

_____

_____

Site #3

Location: _____   Contact: _____

Phone: _____   Fax: _____

E-mail: _____   URL: _____

Number of Guests Site Can Accommodate: _____

Deposit Required: _____   Cancellation Policy: _____

Special Restrictions: _____

On-Site Catering? Y/N   If yes, notes regarding menu and cost: _____

Included: ☐ Tables   ☐ Linens   ☐ Dinnerware   ☐ Chairs   ☐ Kitchen facilities

Beverages Available: _____   Corkage Fee: _____

Cake Baking? Y/N   If yes, notes regarding styles available: _____

Cake Cutting? Y/N   If yes, cake-cutting fee: _____

Music: _____

Is there enough power to handle a band/DJ? Y/N   Is there a dance floor? Y/N

Deposit Required: _____   Cancellation Policy: _____

Special Restrictions: _____

❊ Notes:

_____

_____

_____

The Big Day Schedule

Use this worksheet to organize yourself for the big day. Start in pencil, and see where you've over- or underestimated. Then, revise in pen and follow!

ACTIVITY	TIME
Bride and attendants get dressed	:
Groom and attendants get dressed	:
Photographer takes first pics	:
Transportation for bridal party arrives	3:00 pm
Leave for ceremony	:
Ceremony begins	4:30 pm
Reception begins	7:00 pm
Food and beverages served	:
Music begins	:
Toasts and dancing	:
Cake cutting	:
Bride and groom change outfits	:
Getaway car arrives	:
Bride and groom leave	:

❋Notes:

_____

_____

_____

Guest Accommodations

Once you've set your place, do a little area research for spots where out-of-towners may stay. When finalized, fill this out. Make sure to give a copy of this to your mother, maid/matron of honor, and anyone else designated to be the point person for guests.

Blocks of rooms reserved for wedding at: _____

Hotel: _____

Address: _____

Directions from Airport: _____

_____

Distance from Ceremony Site: _____   Reception Site: _____

Telephone: _____   Fax: _____

Contact: _____

Number of Single Rooms Reserved: _____   Daily Rate: _____

Number of Double Rooms Reserved: _____   Daily Rate: _____

Date Reserved: _____

Terms of Agreement: _____

Payment Procedure: _____

✳ Directions to Ceremony Site:

_____

_____

_____

Other nearby lodging

Hotel: _____

Address: _____

Telephone: _____ Fax: _____

Contact: _____

Daily Rate (single): _____ Daily Rate (double): _____

Hotel: _____

Address: _____

Telephone: _____ Fax: _____

Contact: _____

Daily Rate (single): _____ Daily Rate (double): _____

Hotel: _____

Address: _____

Telephone: _____ Fax: _____

Contact: _____

Daily Rate (single): _____ Daily Rate (double): _____

Notes

Notes

Notes

Notes

Chapter 3

It's Your Party

{Bringing Anti-Bride style to your wedding ambiance}

Know thyself, and the decor and music will follow. As a rule, simple is better, but a little glamour is always good. This chapter discusses what you'll need to make your day a feast for the senses: the flowers, the centerpieces, the invites, the music—all the stuff that shows off your Anti-Bride style.

DO-IT-YOURSELF INVITES

You could choose the formal and fussy engraved invites, sure. But Anti-Brides with flair may opt for one of these DIY options:

INDUSTRIAL CHIC—*Julie Shore, a designer at Gallo Wines, created an invite using an aluminum tube. She inserted the rolled-up invite, directions, and confetti and screwed on the lid. She slapped on the mailing label, and presto!*

YES SIR, SHE'S MY BABY—*Scan in kiddie shots of the two of you side by side; add an apropos quote; print them out on heavy, cream paper; and create a keepsake for your loved ones.*

STORYBOOK WEDDING—*Make your invitation into a little storybook that illustrates how you met—the wedding is the perfect happy ending.*

FAR AND AWAY—*Create an illustrated map invite for your destination wedding.*

CD-ROM INVITATIONS—*Fill your CD with wedding facts, cherished photos, and bridal party information. Perfect for sending to out-of-town guests, close family members, and friends and for keeping as a memento for you and your sweetheart.*

✳ **Anti-Bride Tip** | *E-mail your "Save-the-Date" notices rather than sending by traditional post. This technique comes in especially handy if your wedding is small and if you can include the URL for your wedding Web site, where guests can post their intentions.*

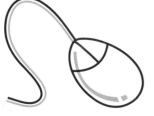

Invitations & Stationery

If you plan to order personalized stationery and invitations, it's best to do it at least six months in advance, if possible. This way, you'll be able to fix any snags in plenty of time.

- ☐ Select and order personal stationery and thank-you notes.
- ☒ Hire designer and printer.
- ☒ Select and order invitations.
- ☒ Select and order announcements.
- ☐ Create and print map and directions.
- ☒ Confirm printing and delivery schedule of invitations, thank-you notes, and other stationery.
- ☐ Hire calligrapher.
- ☒ Purchase stamps.
- ☒ Confirm guest list, including addresses and spellings of names.
- ☐ Select and order monogrammed items such as napkins, wine glasses, etc.
- ☒ Address envelopes.
- ☒ Mail invitations.
- ☐ Write out place cards.

❋ **Anti-Bride Tip** | *You can create a tasteful, yet informative, newsletter giving your guests a heads-up on the wedding festivities. With a little knowledge of Photoshop (or the help from an artistic pal) you can put together a page or two, thanking your guests for coming, explaining the plan for the weekend, and providing creative ideas for spending their downtime.*

Selecting a Printer

Printer #1: Party City

Phone: (315) 488-2913

E-mail:

Price for Invitations (includes response cards and envelopes): $180.25 (for 100)

Thank-You Notes:

Announcements:

Place Cards:

Other:

Printer #2:

Phone:

E-mail:

Price for Invitations (includes response cards and envelopes):

Thank-You Notes:

Announcements:

Place Cards:

Other:

Printer #3:

Phone:

E-mail:

Price for Invitations (includes response cards and envelopes):

Thank-You Notes:

Announcements:

Place Cards:

Other:

Flowers, Centerpieces, etc.

FLOWER LINGO

Know your nosegay from your elbow. Mastering these terms will help you talk the talk with your floral designer to make sure you get exactly what you want.

NOSEGAY: *Small handheld bouquet for mothers of the bride and groom; often used in place of a corsage.*

CORSAGE: *Flower worn on the wrist, lapel, or purse. Conjures up 1950s prom flashbacks.*

BOUTONNIERE: *Flower worn on a man's lapel. All of the wedding party, including ushers, should wear boutonnieres to alert wedding guests that they are part of the wedding.*

BOUQUET: *Flowers carried by the bride and attendants. Bouquets can be loose, airy, tight, round, cascading, monochromatic, concentric, layered, or just-picked. Using these adjectives will help your designer understand what you want.*

ALTARPIECE: *Arrangement often used in the background for indoor wedding photos. Some budget-conscious brides opt for an abundance of candles instead.*

CENTERPIECES: *Arrangements that adorn the reception tables. Guests will spend most of the evening at their tables, so give them something beautiful to look at! Centerpieces range from dramatic flower arrangements to candles and feather boas to large bowls overflowing with fruit.*

CENTERPIECE IDEAS

With tabletops, a little creativity goes a long way, according to Michaela Brockstedt, assistant creative director at Target and former art director at Williams-Sonoma. "One of the things people overlook when dressing tables for a reception area is that simple shapes go a long way and often don't cost as much," she says. "A lot of times, some things may look too plain individually, but once you combine things, it really starts to make a statement."

Make a statement with simple glass vases. Brockstedt says, "Take three or four tall vases of different heights. Add glass pebbles to the bottom of each, and fill them halfway with water. Then, add a few drops of food coloring. Add a single blossom to each vase, and cluster the vases at the center of the table."

Glass bowls add simplicity and elegance to your table. Fill a large glass bowl with water. Place a single exotic blossom in the center and add matching floating candles. Or fill the bowl with lemons, limes, and water, and float gardenias in them.

Floral Elixir. Old medicine bottles in shades of blue and aqua, as well as clear ones, can be picked up inexpensively at flea markets. Group bottles in threes or fours. Fill them with water. Put one bright Gerbera daisy in each.

Anti-Bride Ambiance: Flowers and Beyond

Look to your own backyard or anyone with a garden, lemon trees, or herb patch. You can get bushels of Meyer lemons for your centerpieces or herbs for your chef. A day trip to the mountains might yield some unusual branches, leaves, or berries that could help you create a memorable centerpiece.

❀

Dress up linens with easy-to-find, natural elements. One bride used clippings from a blooming, blue rosemary bush to dress up her linens. She tied the branches to individual linen napkins with a contrasting ribbon for a fragrant tabletop accent.

❀

Collect a variety of mismatched vintage, silver, hotel water pitchers and fill them with colorful cabbage or garden roses from your local flower market. For a lower centerpiece, use the same concept with sugar bowls filled with pansies.

❀

Go to the Chinatown of your nearest city to buy inexpensive black, lacquer vases (red or blue dragons add drama), and put in each vase one perfect white orchid or calla lily from the flower market. Not all vases have to match—unify with black and let the motifs be different.

❀

Collect about 20 coffee cans of the same size. Scan your favorite vintage seed-packet label to size along with a photo of the bride and groom into your computer, and print them out on a color printer. Spray-mount the labels and photos and wrap a label around each can. Put a potted pansy in the middle, and you have cute, country-chic centerpieces.

❀

If you'd rather not use real flowers, consider buying vintage silk and velvet flowers from the 1920s. These also work wonderfully in the hair for that Billie Holiday look. You can find them at Charles Lubin Company in Yonkers, New York, among other places.

❀

Amy Goodman of *In Style* says scattering lavender seeds down the aisle produces an intoxicating scent every time a seed is crushed underfoot.

Take mismatched 1940s-style vases, fill them with flowers of the same color, and put them in the middle of mismatched vintage tablecloths (with bark cloth, scenes of Paris, cabbage roses) for a beautiful, vintage look.

❋

Go through cabinets with grandmothers, mothers, and relatives, and see if there are items you could include in your wedding such as candlesticks, serving dishes, trays, cake servers, and ice tongs. There's nothing like a family heirloom to bring everyone together.

❋

For outdoor ambiance, set up indoor furniture outdoors! Cushy couches, coffee tables, floor pillows, and antique hanging birdcages filled with candles create an unusual atmosphere, says Larissa Thompson of *In Style*.

❋

Lights! Camera! Action! Make sure your wedding is professionally lit. Lighting is one of the most important elements in setting the mood for your guests and making your decor really stand out. If you have a local theater or dance troupe in your town, you probably have a lighting expert. Ask him about gels, scrims, and lighting magic.

❋

Paper or silk lanterns are an inexpensive and colorful way to make a room (and you) glow. Shops such as Pier 1, Urban Outfitters, Target, or your local Chinatown or Indian bazaar will have a variety of choices.

❋ **Anti-Bride Tip |** *Buy a bunch of terracotta pots, paint them silver, and fill with baby rose bushes.*

❋ **Anti-Bride Tip |** *Use topiaries, junior bonsais, or baby magnolia bushes as centerpieces.*

Flowers Worksheet

Use this worksheet to help you focus on your floral vision. Bring with you when checking out florists and flower designers for a handy reminder of your requirements and budget.

FLORAL STYLE:

- ☐ Tightly arranged
- ☐ Natural-looking
- ☐ Elaborate
- ☐ Bold and striking
- ☐ Greens and herbs
- ☐ Exotic flowers (succulents, etc.)

- ☐ Modern and minimal
- ☐ Exotic
- ☐ Subtle
- ☐ Seasonal or local blooms
- ☐ Berries and grasses

Favorite flowers: _____

COLORS:

- ☐ Monochromatic
- ☐ Traditional pastels

- ☐ Multicolored
- ☐ Bold and contemporary

Favorite colors: _____

FLORAL NEEDS:

- ☐ Bridal bouquet (tossing the bouquet)
- ☐ Maid-of-honor's bouquet
- ☐ Bridesmaids' bouquets: ___ (number)
- ☐ Flower girl's flowers (or basket of petals)
- ☐ Nosegays or corsages for moms and grandmothers: ___ (number)
- ☐ Groom's boutonniere
- ☐ Boutonnieres for groomsmen, ushers, dads, and grandfathers: ___ (number)
- ☐ Entry decorations

- ☐ Rose petals for the aisle and/or tossing
- ☐ Additional greenery for the aisle or aisle decoration
- ☐ Altar arrangements: ___ (number)
- ☐ Flower-covered arch or chuppah
- ☐ Reception table centerpieces: ___ (number)
- ☐ Reception buffet table flowers: ___ (number)
- ☐ Arrangement for the placecard table
- ☐ Flowers for the cake table and/or cake decoration

OTHER DECORATION ESSENTIALS:

- ☐ Fabrics
- ☐ Lighting/lamps/lanterns
- ☐ Candles
- ☐ Furniture
- ☐ Other: _____

TOTAL DESIGNER/FLOWER BUDGET: $ _____

Choosing a Florist

QUESTIONS TO ASK ABOUT FLORISTS

* Can you see photographs or live examples of his or her work?
* Does the florist's style and the overall look and feel of the shop jive with your own?
* Does the florist seem knowledgeable about less expensive or creative alternatives, the best flowers for the season, etc.?
* Is the florist familiar with your ceremony and reception sites?
* Will the florist drop off arrangements on the day of your wedding, or will he or she take time to set up and make sure everything is where it should be?
* How many people are on staff, and how many will be assigned to your wedding?
* How many weddings will the florist be designing for the same weekend as your wedding?
* What kind of containers and rental items does the florist offer (vases, plants, arches, candelabras) or do you need to rent them elsewhere?
* Does the fee include cleanup or is this additional? Are flowers donated to charity after the event?

Florist #1:

Company Name: _____ Contact: _____

Phone: _____ Fax: _____

E-mail: _____ URL: _____

Address: _____

Referred by: _____

Style Options: _____

Total Estimated Cost: _____ Deposit Required (by date): _____

Delivery Details (date and time): _____ Delivery Person: _____

Florist #2:

Company Name: _____   Contact: _____

Phone: _____   Fax: _____

E-mail: _____   URL: _____

Address: _____

Referred by: _____

Style Options: _____

Total Estimated Cost: _____   Deposit Required (by date): _____

Delivery Details (date and time): _____   Delivery Person: _____

❋ Tips and Tricks from Floral Design Pro Jolie Fay of Celebrations

✓ If you are looking for more unusual flower combinations, consider vines of stephanotis or clematis, dahlias, thistle, cactus flowers, and other succulents for your bouquets and arrangements (e.g., light blue, pink, and green succulents surrounded by garden roses present an unexpected combination of texture and color).

✓ Always ask your florist to wrap the stems of your bouquets with ribbon, rather than place them in plastic holders. "Plastic feels cheap," says Jolie. "Like wearing polyester from the '70s."

✓ If you're on a budget, use flowers of a single color to unify the room. Use driftwood arranged with candles, gardenias, and seashells. Create runners with wheat grass, and fill with Gerbera daisies.

✓ Use fresh fruit to secure the bases of woody branches and long flower stems in large clear vases.

✓ Create a glamorous runner for long, rectangular tables with white feather boas and long taper candles. Boas can also be used as simple garland decorations on Christmas trees if you are planning a December wedding.

✓ Keep the height of your arrangements in mind—will they obstruct your guests' view or prevent them from mingling?

53

DJ VS. LIVE MUSIC

The flavor of the music at your event sets the mood and vibe and is therefore just as important as the food you serve and the wine you pour. It's the aural backdrop that loosens people up and gets them in a celebratory mood. Try to match the music to the mood you envision. You don't have to hire a designated wedding band. Any band can play at a wedding, although not every band knows how to play wedding favorites. Many brides think that any music outside of big band or Top 40 will not be universally understood by guests. We say, phooey! A great salsa band will have Grandma shakin' her hips, and a swingin' rockabilly band will have Mom and Dad jitterbugging away. Trust in people's ability to adapt and to join in the fun.

Start planning the music and deciding on a reception space simultaneously. Opt for a DJ who'll spin your favorite tunes or live entertainment—maybe a three-piece jazz ensemble, Middle Eastern music with belly dancers, a solo violinist, or the dive-bar band that you see every Friday. The music you choose, whether a live band or DJ plays it, speaks volumes about you and your personal style.

Decide whether you want a DJ, live music, or a little of both—live music for the ceremony, a DJ to spin your favorite disco, swing, or 1980s metal faves for the reception. Next, start sleuthing. The bartender and the DJ at your favorite local bar and the managers of the live-music venues you frequent are good people to ask. Also check out entertainment listings in alternative papers and the local music conservatory.

✳ **Anti-Bride Tip** | *According to muscian and booking agent Natasha Miller, if you have the money and the inclination, you can wow your guests with an international headliner. Get in touch with a local booking agency and plan to spend from $5,000 for a popular older band to $50,000 for a more current crooner.*

✳ **Anti-Bride Tip** | *Check out some local bands in your area. Usually, if they haven't gotten a record deal yet, and you didn't find their name in the wedding directory, their rates will probably be very reasonable.*

✳ **Anti-Bride Tip** | *If you are planning your wedding for early in the week, ask for a lower rate (up to 20 percent) when negotiating the band contract. A wedding will always pay more than a weekday gig, even at a discounted rate.*

LIVE MUSIC

Pro

- ✓ It gets people moving—if you wouldn't be caught dead on a dance floor, you might be inclined to get up and watch the live performance.
- ✓ You can hire a band that specializes in almost any type of music, from swing to country to jazz.
- ✓ The sound quality is always better.
- ✓ A band can manipulate the speed of the songs to fit the mood.
- ✓ In tough economic times, we've found that all bands negotiate.

Con

- ✗ On the average, live bands cost more than DJs.
- ✗ The repertoire is limited to the amount of songs the band knows.
- ✗ They're harder to book than DJs.
- ✗ Songs never sound the same as the original recordings.
- ✗ If the band takes a break, the music stops.
- ✗ If the band has only two volumes—loud and louder—it might feel like a U2 concert, rather than a wedding reception.

DJ

Pro

- ✓ A DJ charges less than a band.
- ✓ A DJ plays the music the way it was recorded. There is no surprise and no fear that singers will try to sing like Aretha Franklin one moment and Barry White the next.
- ✓ The DJ's massive music collection means a broader music range.
- ✓ The DJ is often a natural emcee, but you'll need to make sure of that, particularly with ones that work primarily in discos.
- ✓ There is no reason to have a break in the music.
- ✓ DJs have the equipment to fill a room of any size and with any number of guests with an appropriate amount of sound.

Con

- ✗ You're at the mercy of a one-person show. You'll need to edit the song list; otherwise, you might end up with the standard wedding fare and not your personal tastes.
- ✗ DJs are notorious for bringing along enough equipment for a small army. If you don't want the disco ball or bubble machine, say so before you write the check.
- ✗ If you're going through an agency, read the contracts carefully. Contracts can be misleading in terms of who will really be at your wedding.
- ✗ The DJ may take more effort than a live band to get the crowd engaged.
- ✗ Some guests may think a DJ is too casual for a formal reception.

❊Questions for Talent

You may be working with an agent that represents bands/DJs, or you may work with the talent directly. Either way, it's best to cover your bases by asking them the following questions.

✓ ARE YOU REPRESENTED BY AN AGENCY, OR ARE YOU INDEPENDENT?

✓ WHAT WILL YOU BE WEARING?

✓ DO YOU HAVE THE APPROPRIATE MUSIC AND VARIETY FOR OUR FUNCTION?

CAN I SEE A SONG LIST?

✓ WHAT ARE YOUR SET LENGTHS (BANDS SHOULD PLAY 45 MINUTES ON THE HOUR WITH A 15-MINUTE BREAK)? HOW MANY BREAKS WILL YOU TAKE? HOW LONG? WILL YOU PLAY A CD DURING THIS TIME?

✓ DO YOU CARRY BACKUP GEAR IN CASE OF A POWER FAILURE?

✓ DO YOU PLAY REQUESTS?

✓ DO YOU GENERALLY GET SET UP PRIOR TO THE GUESTS ARRIVING?

✓ ARE YOU LICENSED AND INSURED?

✓ DO YOU USE A CONTRACT?

✓ CAN YOU PROVIDE ME WITH REFERENCES? (ASK FOR 5 TO 10.)

✓ TO DATE, HOW MANY EVENTS HAVE YOU WORKED? (200 OR MORE IS SAFE.)

✓ IS PERFORMING YOUR HOBBY OR A FULL-TIME JOB?

✓ DO YOU EVER PLAY MORE THAN ONE ENGAGEMENT IN A DAY?

✓ HOW MUCH DEPOSIT DO YOU NEED, AND WHAT'S YOUR CANCELLATION AND REFUND POLICY?

✓ WILL SOMEONE BE ABLE TO ACT AS THE EMCEE?

✓ WILL YOU BRING YOUR OWN EQUIPMENT?

✓ ARE YOU REPRESENTED BY AN AGENCY, OR ARE YOU INDEPENDENT?

❊Questions for References

✓ DID THE BAND/DJ SHOW UP ON TIME?

✓ WERE THEY PROFESSIONAL?

✓ DID THEY RETURN PHONE CALLS AND COMMUNICATE WITH YOU WELL?

✓ DID THEY KNOW WHAT YOU WANTED?

✓ DID THEY PLAY A GOOD SET?

✓ DID THEY BREAK DOWN THE EQUIPMENT ON TIME?

✓ HOW DID THEY INTERACT WITH GUESTS? ANY PROBLEMS?

Photography

The photos of your event will last a whole lot longer than the day itself—you'll be looking at that album for years to come. The process of working with your photographer should be organic; pictures should just happen. Your photographer should be a good listener—warm, perceptive, and never formulaic. In the best cases, you should view your photographer as just another friend to hang out and have fun with on your wedding day.

Don't forget to have him or her shoot your rehearsal dinner and build the fee into your contract. Hiring the photographer to do both may result in a reduced rate and will ensure quality and consistency across your wedding album.

Make sure your photographer numbers your proofs in the order they were taken. Then, have the proofs sorted into categories: getting ready, ceremony, portraits, and reception. Most photographers will do this automatically, but it won't hurt to double check. Photographer Karina Marie Diaz supplies her brides with beautiful handmade proof boxes from Paris. Oh la la!

Often, capturing just what you want the way you want it can be a tricky business; here are some suggestions to add some originality, smarts, and creativity when considering photography:

✳ *Get a referral from the dean of your local art college or graduate school. Employ the best documentary photographer, and get a fabulous black-and-white, French New Wave–style wedding album as a result. Mount it in an aluminum binder.*

✳ *Nicole Andersen, of Nicole Andersen Book Arts, suggests working with a bookbinder to custom design your wedding album and memory boxes to hold your cake topper, monogrammed napkin, matchbook, and anything else that you want to save. To ensure that your memories will last forever, use only acid-free paper and pH-neutral adhesives. If you're worried about your budget, add a custom-made album to your registry.*

❋ Karina Marie Diaz asks, "Think about whether you want to have 'getting ready' shots as part of your album. Will you feel comfortable with a male photographer seeing you in your skivvies?"

❋ Hire a (willing) creative, artistic friend to shoot raw footage with a handheld video camera and edit into a fine-art video.

❋ Diaz recommends having your photographer make copies of your favorite engagement photographs to decorate your place cards or thank-you notes. This way everyone will have a picture to remember the day.

❋ Get educated about digital! Going digital is a matter of choosing convenience over quality. Since you don't pay for film processing, printing, or the organization of proofs, the price should be significantly lower than traditional prints.

❋ If you have a talent (graphic design, baking, auto repair) that you can "trade" with a photographer, perhaps you can work out a deal. Many artists are accustomed to working for trade, and it certainly never hurts to ask.

Delegation Patrol

DELEGATION PATROL: SHARE THE LOVE

Your binder runneth over with details: phone numbers, fabric samples, brochures, bands, venues, and menus. Every bride who's been through it will tell you it's a full-time job, and as any good project manager knows, you can't do everything. Worry about being fabulous on your wedding day—not picking up corsages and wedding favors. Leave that to your pals. Remember you're the CEO of your wedding. As long as you have the vision and delegation abilities, you'll be a smashing success. Here's a checklist that will help you run your wedding like a pro.

Make a master spreadsheet of everything that must be done for the big day. Put a check next to the tasks that you absolutely must do yourself.

- ☐ Write down the names of all of your friends and family members who may want to get involved. Do they have special talents that could contribute to your wedding? Make a note of them so you remember when assigning tasks.
- ☐ When assigning responsibilities, make sure you have dependable people who have a clear idea of what you want. The last thing you need is a late-breaking emergency or disappointment.
- ☐ Stand firm on your decisions. It's great that Aunt Sally wants to book hotels and transportation, but is she going to get around to it? It may be hard to say no; but, remember, this is your perfect day.
- ☐ Create an e-mailable spreadsheet to reduce redundancies in phone calls. Insist that people contact you by e-mail, and turn off your phones.

❋**Anti-Bride Tip** | *Stay in control. Put on your project manager cap. Make sure you are firm if someone starts doing tasks without consulting you—or requests a task that you would rather do or that would be more appropriate for someone else. Thank the person for the offer, but tell them it's been taken care of. It may cause issues in the future if they do some thing you are unhappy with or, worse yet, don't complete the task at all.*

❋**Anti-Bride Tip** | *There are things you probably shouldn't delegate to a friend. The important things on your big day—food, music, cake baking, dressmaking, and emcee responsibilities— should be left to pros. This way, you've got contracts and expectations, and if there are problems, you can deal with them on a professional level without ruffling any feathers and harming relationships.*

Task Assignments

❋ *Creative tasks—*calligraphy for the invitations; designing the centerpieces; ideas for decoration or wedding favors.

WHO: _____ Deanna _____

❋ *Sewing tasks—*headpieces, any sewing for favors, tablecloths, etc.

WHO: _____ Baba _____

❋ *Number-crunching tasks—*setting up a financial spreadsheet; assisting in breaking down expenses.

WHO: _____ Me! _____

❋ *Project-management tasks—*let an assistant plan and conquer on your behalf. Give her a list of all your dependable, detail-oriented friends, and have her split up the tasks from there. Your assistant should handle tasks like picking up corsages, tuxedos, gifts from the reception, flowers, and the favors. When you follow up on all those nitty-gritty details, you only have to deal with one point of contact.

WHO: _____

❋ *Handy-household tasks—*house-sitting or walking and feeding pets while you're on your honey-moon, or babysitting during events that don't involve children.

WHO: _____

wedding night!

❋

WHO: _____

❋

WHO: _____

Gift Registry

Even if you're not keen on the idea of registering for gifts, it's always a good idea. Your friends and family will get you something, and it might as well be something that you want! You don't have to limit yourself to flatware; consider registering for anything from power tools to cooking classes to a second car. Use these lists here to check off the things most important to you.

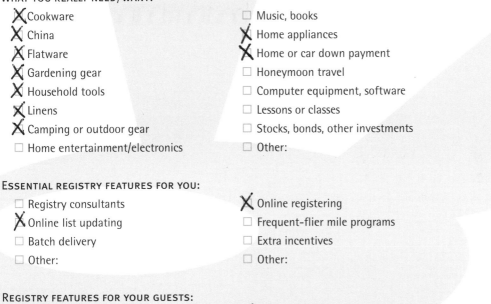

WHAT YOU REALLY NEED/WANT:

- [x] Cookware
- [x] China
- [x] Flatware
- [x] Gardening gear
- [x] Household tools
- [x] Linens
- [x] Camping or outdoor gear
- [ ] Home entertainment/electronics

- [ ] Music, books
- [x] Home appliances
- [x] Home or car down payment
- [ ] Honeymoon travel
- [ ] Computer equipment, software
- [ ] Lessons or classes
- [ ] Stocks, bonds, other investments
- [ ] Other:

ESSENTIAL REGISTRY FEATURES FOR YOU:

- [ ] Registry consultants
- [x] Online list updating
- [ ] Batch delivery
- [ ] Other:

- [x] Online registering
- [ ] Frequent-flier mile programs
- [ ] Extra incentives
- [ ] Other:

REGISTRY FEATURES FOR YOUR GUESTS:

- [ ] Toll-free phone ordering
- [x] Local, in-person access via chain stores
- [ ] Other:

- [x] E-mail ordering
- [ ] National access via catalogs
- [ ] Other:

REGISTRY TIPS

- ✓ *Always consider price. Be sure to register for gifts in a range of different prices, so every guest will be able to afford something. The average amount spent is $50 to $150.*
- ✓ *Keep it simple. Don't drive yourself crazy keeping track of multiple registries. Look for a registry or store that has most of what you want.*
- ✓ *Keep convenience in mind. All your guests should be able to access your registry online, 24-7.*
- ✓ *Update your list and expand when necessary. Keep tabs on what gets purchased, and be sure to add more items once all that remain are cheap (but useful!) gadgets and expensive appliances.*

Gift Registry Contact Info

Registry #1: Bed Bath & Beyond

Address: 3597 W. Genesee St., Syr, NY 13219

Phone: (315) 488-4535

Contact:

URL: bedbathandbeyond.con

Appointment Date:

Time:

Description/Notes:

Registry #2: Target

Address:

Phone:

Contact:

URL:

Appointment Date:

Time:

Description/Notes:

Registry #3: Khol's

Address:

Phone:

Contact:

URL:

Appointment Date:

Time:

Description/Notes:

✳Questions for Registry Consultant

✓ WHO WILL YOUR MAIN CONTACT BE?

✓ WHAT RANGE OF PRODUCTS DO YOU CARRY AND WHAT BRANDS?

✓ WILL YOUR REGISTRY BE ACCESSIBLE ONLINE? CAN GUESTS MAKE PURCHASES ONLINE? CAN YOUR REGISTRY LIST BE FAXED TO GUESTS SO THAT THEY CAN ORDER BY PHONE?

✓ HOW DOES THE REGISTRY KEEP TRACK OF WHAT IS PURCHASED? HOW OFTEN IS IT UPDATED?

✓ WHAT IS THE RETURN POLICY? CAN YOU RETURN UNWANTED ITEMS FOR CREDIT OR EXCHANGES?

✓ IS THERE A TIME LIMIT IN WHICH YOU MUST RETURN THE GIFTS?

✓ IS THERE A COMPLETION PROGRAM WHERE YOU ARE ABLE TO PURCHASE, AT A DISCOUNT, GIFTS THAT YOUR GUESTS DID NOT GET? FOR HOW LONG AFTER YOUR WEDDING IS THIS OFFER AVAILABLE?

✓ HOW LONG AFTER YOUR WEDDING WILL YOUR REGISTRY LIST BE KEPT ACTIVE? (IT SHOULD BE ACCESSIBLE FOR AT LEAST ONE YEAR.)

Announcement Worksheet

Use this as a template if you and your sweetie decide to formally "announce" your nuptials.

Publication: _____

Address: _____ *URL:* _____

Contact: _____

Phone: _____ *Fax:* _____

Deadline: _____

_____ AND _____
(bride's first, middle, last name)   (groom's first, middle, last name)

WERE MARRIED AT _____ IN _____ .
(name of church, synagogue, other location)   (city/town, state)

THE BRIDE IS THE DAUGHTER OF MR. AND MRS. _____ OF _____ .
(last name)   (their city/town, state)

SHE GRADUATED FROM _____ AND IS A/AN _____ AT _____ .
(college/university)   (job title)   (employer)

THE BRIDEGROOM IS THE SON OF MR. AND MRS. _____ OF _____ ,
(last name)   (their city/town, state)

GRADUATED FROM _____ AND IS A/AN _____ AT _____ .
(college/university)   (job title)   (employer)

THE COUPLE WILL LIVE IN _____ AFTER A TRIP TO _____ .
(city/town, state)   (honeymoon location)

BRIDE'S NOTABLE ACHIEVEMENTS: _____

GROOM'S NOTABLE ACHIEVEMENTS: _____

Notes

✳ Anti-Bride Tip | *Rent a photo booth! Instead of signing a traditional guest book, guests can take a goofy photo of themselves and place it in the enclosed vellum envelope with their names and a note. Make sure to stock the booth with lots of props (silly hats, boas, costume jewelry).*

Notes

_____

_____

_____

_____

_____

_____

_____

_____

_____

_____

_____

_____

_____

_____

_____

_____

❋ Anti-Bride Tip | *She She Events says: "We had a couple that incorporated a drawing that the groom's little sister drew of them into their save-the-date, invitation, program, favor, and even a guide to San Francisco for out-of-town guests. The child's drawing was charming and personal."*

Notes

Notes

Chapter 4

Eat, Drink, Be Married

{Choosing food, wine, Champagne, and more}

What you wear and the glow you emanate will be remembered by all but your family and hubby for maybe a week. The food and drink, well, that's another story. Even guys remember what was served at weddings. Memorable standouts—oysters served in an ice-filled rowboat in Cape Cod, crab cakes by the Annapolis docks, Smithfield ham on buttermilk biscuits in the Deep South—are etched into your guests' minds. This is not always a good thing, especially if the food leaves something to be desired. How many weddings have you, dear Anti-Bride, attended where they ran out of a main course, and you were left with the dregs of the chafing dish? Your hospitality and generosity are most evident in the table you set. Quality and quantity are what matter. Timeliness and efficiency run a close second. Don't spend a king's ransom on your spread—just make sure you can truly host those you've invited, or reduce your list to a point where you can.

Whether you are hosting a sit-down meal or a reception with heavy hors d'oeuvres, start sampling the wares of people you respect. Choose your caterer fairly early in the game. Rely on recommendations from friends, chefs, or others in the industry. When you're in initial discussions, have the following information ready:

- ❊ YOUR BUDGET!
- ❊ LOCATION OF THE WEDDING
- ❊ PICTURES FROM MAGAZINES YOU LIKE
- ❊ THEME OF THE WEDDING
- ❊ THE STYLE YOU ARE AFTER
- ❊ YOUR FAVORITE FLAVORS

APPETIZER IDEAS

Treat your guests to a spread of high-concept food with a bargain-basement price tag. According to New York City caterer Peg Devlin, the money you spend has more to do with the preparation and presentation of the food and less to do with the actual ingredients. Following is a model appetizer menu (all have been tested and have received a big thumbs-up!):

- ✓ Stuffed tomatoes with various fillings
- ✓ Croustades with various fillings
- ✓ Ham biscuits
- ✓ Crabcakes with cucumber-tartar sauce
- ✓ Caprice skewers
- ✓ Tomato tartlets
- ✓ Prosciutto-wrapped shrimp
- ✓ Salmon pinwheels
- ✓ Sun-dried tomato spread
- ✓ Pork skewers
- ✓ Chicken satay with peanut sauce

BON APPÉTIT

"There is really no trick to throwing a good party," says chef Max Braud of Le Zinc Brasserie in San Francisco. "You merely need to serve food that people like to eat and keep it very simple." We couldn't agree more! At Carolyn and Laurent's Paris wedding, it was an *affaire de famille*. His mother buttered baguettes and spread caviar on rounds. His dad bought the largest pâté and an array of cheeses at the open market. His cousin, a baker at the Hôtel Le Crillon, made the cake. The wine was from the cellar, the mustard rabbit was in a casserole dish, and everyone enjoyed each other's company in a luxurious, candlelit atmosphere.

Southern Living

New Orleans folks know how to throw a fête: jambalaya, red beans and rice, mint juleps, pulled pork, and a Southern-style cake room. At homespun Southern weddings, women in the family (and friends and neighbors) bake their finest. What results is a dedicated cake room, where every cake and confection imaginable is on display. For libations, fresh squeezed lemonade with bourbon and mint is served.

TAPAS & TIRAMISÙ

You don't have to have only one type of food under the umbrella we call "theme." If you love the idea of a Spanish tapas bar, Mexican margaritas, sushi appetizers, and tiramisù for dessert, go ahead. Serve your favorite foods.

Anti-Bride Tip | *To cut costs, says caterer Catherine Kitz, serve only one entrée. Two meal options means two lines of servers and two chefs. She also brings a vegetarian alternative for 10 percent of the guests.*

Anti-Bride Tip | *If your wedding is outdoors, serve room-temperature dishes—salmon vinaigrette, pasta salad, salad niçoise, grilled chicken, risotto salad—to cut costs on rented hot plates, heat lamps, and Sterno dishes.*

Anti-Bride Tip | *Little touches count. Michaela Brockstedt suggests that before the reception, greet guests with something, whether it's a glass of champagne or some little nibbles. It's a nice way to put a little flair into a wedding. One beautiful idea: serve little Belgian dark chocolate cups filled with raspberry liquor on silver trays to guests while they're waiting for the reception to start or dinner to be completed.*

CATERING CONTRACTS

Many catering contracts are extremely "line-itemed," says caterer Catherine Kitz. This is mainly to ensure that there are no questions when the bride signs on the dotted line. Here are a few examples of what the contract might spell out:

✓ NUMBER OF STAFF THAT WILL BE WORKING. THE RULE OF THUMB IS ONE WAITER PER 15 GUESTS FOR A BUFFET AND ONE WAITER PER 10 GUESTS FOR A SIT-DOWN.
✓ NUMBER OF HOURS STAFF WILL BE WORKING.
✓ PER PERSON PRICE ON FOOD, LINENS, PLACE SETTINGS, GLASSWARE, ETC.
✓ THE KIND OF SETUP ACHIEVABLE WITHIN A CERTAIN PERIOD OF TIME.

✱ Anti-Bride Tip | *Do things out of order. Have cocktails and appetizers first, then the ceremony, and then the rest of the party. You'll be able to relax and mingle with your friends. Your guests are more likely to feel included in your wedding, rather than like they're watching a staged production.*

BUBBLY STRATEGIES

Niall McCallum, a rep for an Italian importer, says, that nowadays, good-quality sparkling wines are made worldwide. To get the best deal, buy in December when the bulk of the supplier's business takes place. Or check out California and western producers—like Gloria Ferrer, Mumm Cuvée Napa, Gruet, and Domaine Ste. Michelle. All are available for less than $20 per bottle.

Alternatives include Italy's *prosecco*. Its crisp, refreshing, and moderately low-alcohol character makes it a perfect toasting wine. Good producers—Canella, Mionetto, Nino Franco, among others—are from Conegliano and Valdobbiadene; bottles are generally under $20. Chenin Blanc, a grape from France's Loire Valley, can exhibit rounder styles of peach and pear with wonderful aromatics. Examples under $20 are Domaine des Baumard, Charles de Fere, and Monmousseau. Thinner and crisper with a high acidity, *cava*, from Spain, is another option. Two popular examples are Freixenet and Codorníu.

According to caterer Catherine Kitz, typically, don't rule out a full bar, thinking beer and wine is a more cost-effective alternative. The reason? One bottle of wine serves five, while one bottle of booze serves 30 to 40; however, both bottles are about the same price.

❋ Basic Bar (Peter Gowdy, bartender, Tony Nik's in San Francisco's North Beach)

✓ Vodka: Absolut, Stolichnaya, or Ketel One

✓ Gin: Tanqueray, Bombay Sapphire

✓ Rum: Bacardi

✓ Tequila: Cuervo White, Herradura

✓ Scotch: Dewar's

✓ Cordial: Triple Sec

✓ Mixers: sour mix, soda, tonic, Coke, ginger ale

✓ Juices: cranberry, orange, grapefruit

✓ Garnishes: lemons, limes, oranges

❋ **Anti-Bride Tip |** *Here's a great presentation for little sips: Fill a rectangular box with water and position wooden dowels vertically in the water. Let freeze. Remove dowels and replace with shot glasses, and serve your favorite hors d'oeuvre in between!*

When Guests Have a Little Too Much

When there's access to free booze, there's always a notorious suspect who doesn't know when to say when. To keep the day as stress-free as possible, do a little preparation, and have a game plan. Designate a family member as a point person. Let your bartender know drinks should not be too strong—open bars can be dangerous. Enlist a few friends to feel out the crowd when the reception is nearing the end. Guests who seem a little tipsy should be told that out of concern, a ride will be arranged for them.

Choosing a Caterer

QUESTIONS TO ASK ABOUT CATERERS

✓ Does the caterer specialize in a particular food or service style? (Ask for sample menus from past weddings and parties.)

✓ Will the caterer arrange a tasting of the foods you are interested in serving?

✓ What is the average price per head (food, linens, place settings, glassware, etc.)? Are costs itemized depending on the foods you select? (If so, ask for printed price sheets.) Or is there a flat-rate fee that is all-inclusive? (If so, what would that include?)

✓ How involved is the caterer in a typical reception? Do they cue the band, tell you when to cut the cake, and adjust the serving schedule if necessary? (If your caterer or site manager isn't willing to do this, you'll probably want to hire a coordinator for the day.)

✓ Who will be your main contact? Will this same person also help plan and oversee the meal service on your wedding day? (Working with one person is most desirable.)

✓ Is the caterer working any other weddings or large parties on the same weekend of your wedding?

✓ Is the caterer able to provide tables, chairs, linens, and dinnerware? If required, will he or she arrange for rentals?

✓ Does the caterer set the tables (including the arrangement of place cards and favors)?

✓ Will the caterer provide a wait staff? If so, how many servers for your wedding? (Rule of thumb is one waiter per 10 to 15 guests.) How many hours will the staff be working? What will the servers be wearing?

✓ Where will food be prepared? Will the caterer need to set up a field kitchen instead of, or in addition to, the on-site facilities? Is there an additional fee for this setup?

✓ Does the caterer work with fresh or frozen food?

✓ Do they have a license? (A license means that the caterer has met health department standards and has liability insurance; just be sure the license covers liquor if you are planning to have a bar.)

✓ Can the caterer provide alcohol, or is the bar your responsibility? If you provide it, is there a corkage fee? How and when should you get the alcohol to the caterer? If the caterer provides it, does he or she have a flexible wine list (i.e., can you make special requests)? Is the alcohol purchased up front or on consignment (consignment means that the caterer can return unused quantities for credit)?

✓ How much time does the caterer need to set up? What kind of setup is achievable within a given period of time?

Choosing a Caterer

Use this worksheet to gather info and compare services from different caterers. When you make your choice, be sure to input the winner into The Phone Book at the back of the planner.

Caterer #1

Company name: _____   Contact: _____

Phone: _____   Fax: _____

E-mail: _____   URL: _____

Address: _____

Menu options: _____

☐ Brunch   ☐ Lunch   ☐ Hors d'oeuvres only   ☐ Dinner

Buffet: _____

Sit-down: _____

Beverages and food: _____

☐ Wine   ☐ Champagne   ☐ Open bar   ☐ Espresso bar   ☐ Other

Servers included in price? Y/N   Bartender included in price? Y/N

Require on-site kitchen? Y/N   Table/flatware and serving dishes included? Y/N

Additional fees (such as corkage, cake-cutting, overtime)? Y/N $

Attire: _____   Number of staff: _____

Cost of food per guest: _____   Cost of drinks per guest: _____

Final headcount (needed by date): _____

Deposit required (by date): _____

TOTAL ESTIMATED COST:

Caterer #2

Company name: _____   Contact: _____

Phone: _____   Fax: _____

E-mail: _____   URL: _____

Address: _____

Menu options: _____

☐ Brunch   ☐ Lunch   ☐ Hors d'oeuvres only   ☐ Dinner

Buffet: _____

Sit-down: _____

Beverages and food: _____

☐ Wine   ☐ Champagne   ☐ Open bar   ☐ Espresso bar   ☐ Other

Servers included in price? Y/N   Bartender included in price? Y/N

Require on-site kitchen? Y/N   Table/flatware and serving dishes included? Y/N

Additional fees (such as corkage, cake-cutting, overtime)? Y/N $ _____

Attire: _____   Number of staff: _____

Cost of food per guest: _____   Cost of drinks per guest: _____

Final headcount (needed by date): _____

Deposit required (by date): _____

TOTAL ESTIMATED COST:

Caterer #3

Company name: _____ Contact: _____

Phone: _____ Fax: _____

E-mail: _____ URL: _____

Address: _____

Menu options: _____

☐ Brunch ☐ Lunch ☐ Hors d'oeuvres only ☐ Dinner

Buffet: _____

Sit-down: _____

Beverages and food: _____

☐ Wine ☐ Champagne ☐ Open bar ☐ Espresso bar ☐ Other

Servers included in price? Y/N Bartender included in price? Y/N

Require on-site kitchen? Y/N Table/flatware and serving dishes included? Y/N

Additional fees (such as corkage, cake-cutting, overtime)? Y/N $ _____

Attire: _____ Number of staff: _____

Cost of food per guest: _____ Cost of drinks per guest: _____

Final headcount (needed by date): _____

Deposit required (by date): _____

TOTAL ESTIMATED COST:

Wedding Cake

Whether a towering facade of white-frosted architecture or a table of the neighbors' best recipes, wedding cakes are symbols of a decadent celebration.

Baker Emily Dolan says the high cost of a wedding cake has more to do with the cake decoration than the cake itself. Her advice for budget-conscious brides? "Stick to simple cakes. You get more bang for your buck that way."

✻ Anti-Bride Tip | *If planning an outdoor wedding, you should try to keep the cake indoors or in the shade. It's best to refrigerate the cake or put it in a freezer, if possible, until the reception.*

There's no "typical" wedding cake, says Susan Morgan, owner of Elegant Cheesecakes, whose cakes range from her specialty wedding cheesecakes and tiramisù cakes to individual desserts. Things brides should consider when choosing a wedding cake:

✻ **Favorite flavors.** Are you a chocoholic, or do you love cream cheese or fruit?
✻ **Favorite desserts.** Are you more hot fudge sundae, or mixed berry tart?
✻ **Looks or taste.** Do you want a more elaborate presentation or a more expensive filling?
✻ **Budget.** The wide range in choices means an equally wide range of prices.
✻ **The wedding space.** It affects the ingredients the baker uses.

And how about toppers? Kay Dillion, a cake baker, creates whimsical shapes (hearts, flowers, butterflies) with wires and Swarovski crystal to decorate the tops of her cakes. Other suggestions: crystal beads; a monogram made out of handmade, vintage sequined,or silk flowers; a black-and-white snapshot framed in icing.

Cakewalk: A Frosting Glossary

Butter cream: Creamy, light-tasting frosting made of meringue, butter, and vanilla. Melts in hot, humid weather. A no-no for outdoor summer weddings.

Ganache: Chocolate truffle filling made of chocolate and cream whisked together.

Fondant: Sugar paste that is rolled out and draped over the cake to create a porcelain-perfect, pliable shell.

White chocolate: Melted white chocolate kneaded with corn syrup and fondant to give it elasticity.

Cake design elements: Arches, ropes, bowls, balls, fruits, elements from your dress or invitations.

Wedding Cake Ideas

Ah, the cake. This is your chance to design the dessert of your dreams. So, go for it—just remember that it should taste as good as it looks, says Sonja Hong of Butterfly Cakes! Generally, you can take some time deciding on a baker and cake design, even waiting until the last months before the wedding. Keep in mind that if you have your heart set on a well-known cake designer, you'll need to book as far in advance as possible.

STYLE:
- ☐ Traditional
- ☐ Modern
- ☐ Ornate
- ☐ Architectural

PRESENTATION:
- ☐ Sheet cake
- ☒ Tiered
- ☐ Tiered with columns
- ☐ Number of tiers: _____

SHAPE:
- ☒ Round
- ☐ Square
- ☐ Something other than a cake (i.e., cupcakes, pies, etc.)
- ☐ Other shape: _____

DECORATION:
- ☐ Fresh flowers
- ☒ Handmade sugar flowers
- ☐ Other: _____
- ☐ Topper: _____

USE:
- ☐ As a decorative centerpiece
- ☒ As the primary dessert
- ☐ For the traditional cake-cutting ceremony

Flavors I Like:

Colors I Like:

Design/Theme Ideas:

Number of Slices Needed:

GROOM'S CAKE: ☐ YES   ☐ NO

Groom's cake flavor and design ideas:

Number of slices needed:

TOTAL CAKE BUDGET: $_____

✳Questions for the Baker

1. WILL THE BAKER CREATE A CUSTOM CAKE, OR MUST YOU CHOOSE A SPECIFIC STYLE?
   (Ask to see photos, as well as actual cakes, if possible.)

2. DOES HE OR SHE USE FRESH INGREDIENTS? (I.E., FRESH VS. CANNED FRUIT, FARM-FRESH BUTTER, ETC.)

3. WHAT KINDS OF FILLINGS AND CAKE FLAVORS ARE AVAILABLE?

4. HOW FAR IN ADVANCE WILL YOUR CAKE BE PREPARED?

5. WILL THE SAME PERSON BE BAKING, DESIGNING, AND DECORATING YOUR CAKE? HOW MANY PEOPLE WORK WITH THE DESIGNER?

6. HOW MANY WEDDING CAKES DOES THE BAKER MAKE IN A WEEKEND?

7. IF YOU WOULD LIKE TO DECORATE YOUR CAKE WITH FRESH BLOOMS, WILL THE DESIGNER WORK WITH YOUR FLORIST, OR WILL YOU BE RESPONSIBLE FOR GETTING THE FLOWERS?

8. ARE THE CAKES PRICED BY THE SLICE OR BY THE CAKE? ARE DIFFERENT FILLINGS AND FROSTINGS PRICED DIFFERENTLY? WILL THERE BE EXTRA COSTS IF THE CAKE IS CUSTOM-MADE?

9. IS THE CAKE'S TOP TIER INCLUDED IN THE PRICE, OR IS IT EXTRA?
   (Some bakers will include it for free or give you a coupon good for a free one-year-anniversary cake.)

10. IS THE BAKER LICENSED BY THE STATE HEALTH DEPARTMENT?

11. WILL THE BAKER HAND-DELIVER AND SET UP THE CAKE? IF NOT, WHOM WILL HE OR SHE HIRE? IS THERE AN EXTRA CHARGE FOR THE DELIVERY?

Baker #1

Company name: **Mario's Bakery** Contact: **Mario or Linda**

Phone: **(315) 452-3306** Fax: **(315) 452-3307**

E-mail: URL:

Address: **505 N. Main St., N. Syr, NY 13212**

Style and flavor options:

Cake-cutting service? Y/**N** Cake-cutting fee:

Total estimated cost: **$350 plus $20 delivery fee** Deposit required (by date): **Upon order**

Delivery/Pickup (date and time) **10/1, 5:30pm** Delivery person:

Baker #2

Company name: Contact:

Phone: Fax:

E-mail: URL:

Address:

Style and flavor options:

Cake-cutting service? Y/N Cake-cutting fee:

Total estimated cost: Deposit required (by date):

Delivery/Pickup (date and time) Delivery person:

Notes

_____

_____

_____

_____

_____

_____

_____

_____

_____

_____

_____

_____

_____

_____

_____

_____

_____

_____

Anti-Bride Tip | *To save money, call the cake anything else but a wedding cake (birthday cake, anniversary cake). They won't get caught up in the wedding hoopla and will just bake you something tasty. Saves you money, but also looks fabulous.*

Notes

_____

_____

_____

_____

_____

_____

_____

_____

_____

_____

_____

_____

_____

_____

❋**Anti-Bride Tip** | *Portion control: Every standard bottle of wine yields approximately five glasses. Most caterers use the 2:1 ratio of reds to whites. Sparkling serves six to seven guests, because of the size of flutes. Count on refills.*

Notes

Notes

✳ Anti-Bride Tip| *A savvy caterer will prepare a food basket to take with you, containing samples of all the food served, cake, and Champagne. With all the activity, chances are, this will be the first time you've tasted all your gourmet goodies.*

Chapter 5

Sparkle Plenty
{Putting your loveliest face forward}

We all want to look stunning on our big day, and this means taking stock in whatcha got and filling in the blanks for whatcha don't. Having gone down to your fighting weight, you could be wearing the latest John Galliano confection, but if your face is embalmed in a makeup mask, you run the risk of looking like a soap-opera bride. No matter what you've seen in the magazines, more is never better—and the photographs don't come out more vivid if you pile it on. Wear what feels comfortable. Trust yourself and the most stylish gal you know, and then do the final editing. If you need inspiration, look in beauty mags and find a model who most closely resembles your coloring and facial structure—the accompanying text usually lists products used. If there is a Sephora store in your town, you're in luck—it's a candy store of try-on glamour with a no-pressure sales team (and all products are available online at *www.sephora.com*).

When you're thinking about hair, think about climate: Are you in the humid South, the foggy Bay Area, or in windy Chicago? What you put in your hair and how you wear it should track with the weather. We don't want that sculpting wax melting into your tiara or that precision updo blowing out in the wind!

Change is good, but not two weeks before the big day—don't try on any new looks, techniques, or diets right before your wedding. Razor-thin brows or chunky hair streaks might not jive with your natural beauty. Remember, you want your family and friends to recognize you, not worry that you've entered a witness protection program. Fad diets can cause skin allergies or, worse, weaken your immune system to a point where you become ill. The ideal look is the best version of you that's possible: the most glowing, pretty, and relaxed gal that ever sashayed down the aisle, even if you're shaking an extra five pounds.

For that healthy glow, Jeanine Lobell of Stila Cosmetics suggests good old-fashioned exercise in lieu of cosmetic shimmer creams, which make your face look oily. Only use on the collarbones. She loves the modern classic look—defined eyebrows, beigey sparkly eye shadow with matching eyeliner, and shimmer lipstick. She also says not to follow every trend: "Some trends are hip, but they aren't all pretty."

Get a trial run of what your hairdo will look like in advance of the wedding, says Kellie Little, owner of Zindagi hair salon in San Francisco. Bring a dress of similar neckline and color, the jewels, and, if possible, the headpiece. Tight, constructed updos are formal and nighttime; messy updos are sexy, outdoorsy, and daytime. Hair considerations: formality of wedding, time of day, climate, what looks best on you, how your hair behaves with your headpiece. Let your stylist know the wedding location—indoor hair behaves differently than outdoor hair and needs different styling products. If you're getting married out of town and want your hair styled, have a consultation beforehand.

✳ **Anti-Bride Tip** | *At your wedding, have handy a facial spritzer that can be used throughout the day to hydrate skin.*

ANTI-BRIDE MAKEUP SUGGESTIONS

Eyes: Pink-and-gold shimmer on lids is a universally gorgeous look.

Skin: Cleanse with rose water and glycerin (available at most drugstores). It's an inexpensive but moisturizing clarifier. Lose all the alpha hydroxy acid (AHA) cleansers and creams, which can be harsh on your skin. Using a body butter the night before will make your skin the softest ever in the morning.

Lips: Keep colored lipstick from budging by moisturizing around the mouth. Pat with silicone cream (such as Fresh Face Primer by Fresh) to fill in lines. Put on a coat of color. Place a tissue over the lips, and pat loose powder through the tissue. Apply another layer of color. Seal the whole deal with a lip sealer.

Scent: To keep your sensual scent going all day long, use essential oils. Since they are not alcohol based, they don't dissipate so quickly.

Eyebrows: Have your eyebrows done (tweezed or colored) a week before the wedding. If you are on Accutane, no waxing you will blister! Take an old mascara brush, run it under water and run it across your eyebrows. Your brows will look more natural than using pencil.

✳ **Anti-Bride Tip** | *Jane Iredale of Iredale Mineral Cosmetics suggests you consult an expert to choose colors that are best for your skin tone. Plan a makeup rehearsal, complete with a Polaroid, to try them out. See how they translate onto film.*

✳ **Anti-Bride Tip** | *Don't wash your hair the day of your wedding. "Two-day dirty" (wedding being the second day) is the optimal styling condition. Use a colorless henna mudpack a few days before for added body.*

ANTI-BRIDE EMERGENCY KIT

- ☑ ~~TWO BOTTLES OF NAIL POLISH (A CLEAR ONE FOR NYLON RUNS; ANOTHER FOR YOUR NAILS)~~
- ☑ ~~EXTRA STOCKINGS~~
- ☐ STATIC GUARD
- ☐ MIRROR
- ☐ COMB AND BRUSH
- ☐ SAFETY PINS
- ✗ DEODORANT
- ☐ BENEFIT'S SHE-LAQ FOR KEEPING YOUR EYEBROWS AND LIPSTICK IN PLACE.
- ☑ ~~NAIL FILE~~
- ☐ ANTACIDS AND EXCEDRIN
- ✗ CLEAR TAPE
- ☐ BABY POWDER
- ☐ LOTION
- ✗ SPRAY SPOT REMOVER
- ☐ HAIR DRYER
- ☐ CURLING IRON
- ☐ SANITARY NEEDS
- ✗ PHONE LIST OF VENDORS
- ☐ CELL PHONE
- ☐ PLASTIC BAGS
- ☐ SNACKS
- ☐ CHALK FOR TOUCHING UP SHIRTS, BLOUSES, AND DRESSES
- ☐ DENTAL FLOSS

DUWOP STANDARD EMERGENCY KIT

❋ **Cristina Bartolucci and Laura DeLuisa of DuWop cosmetics recommend:**

- ☐ *Altoids, mints, or spray breath-freshener*
- ☐ *Bobby pins*
- ☐ *Baby wipes—wardrobe experts use them to remove makeup stains. Use them as makeup removers, or lightly trail one through the hair to eliminate flyaways.*
- ☐ *Lip gloss with a touch of color*
- ☐ *Blotting papers and compact powder*
- ☐ *Visine—not only gets the red out of eyes, but also doubles as a quick zit fix! (If you have time, freeze a drop and let it melt on your zit for an even more miraculous result.)*
- ☐ *Tissue travel pack*

KITCHEN-CUPBOARD RECIPES FOR NATURAL BEAUTY

✳ **From Diane Irons, 911 Beauty Secrets:**

BLEMISH-BUSTING MASK: Mix 1/2 teaspoon turmeric with just enough water to form a paste. Apply to blemishes. Leave overnight.

CHOCOLATE BODY WRAP: Mix a 1/4 cup honey with 3/4 cup cocoa powder. Heat the mixture in the microwave until warm but comfortable. Apply all over body. Rinse off in the shower after 20 minutes.

ORANGE PEEL FOR SKIN TONE: Combine 1 peeled, chopped orange with 2 tablespoons coarse sea salt. Massage mixture over dry skin. Leave on five minutes. Rinse well.

CELLULITE PASTE: Blend 1/2 cup coffee beans with 1/2 cup salt, 1 teaspoon kelp, and 4 tablespoons olive oil until it forms a paste. Apply the mixture over the dimpled skin. Gently rub in circular motion with hands or loofah. Rinse well and vigorously pat dry.

✳ **From Donna Maria, founder of the Handmade Beauty Network:**

LIP SOFTENER: Mix 1 tablespoon ground oats with 1 teaspoon olive oil, 1 teaspoon honey, and 1 tablespoon rose water or green tea. Grind in a coffee or spice mill. Form a paste, apply to lips, and leave on two minutes. Rinse with warm water.

HAND SOFTENER: Mix together 1 small egg yolk, 1 teaspoon honey, 2 tablespoons olive oil, 1 tablespoon sugar, and 2 drops lemon essential oil. Stir the mixture to evenly combine the ingredients. Massage into clean, damp hands. Leave on five minutes. Rinse with warm water.

SOOTHING SOAK FOR EYES: Soak herbal tea bags (green tea and rooibos tea work well) in hot water to moisten the herbs. Squeeze liquid out of tea bag. Chill in the refrigerator for 15 minutes, and then place them over your eyes as you relax in a bubble bath.

✳ **Anti-Bride Tip |** *Make a paste of baking soda and water, and pat it on the face. It absorbs oil and brightens the complexion.*

✳ **Anti-Bride Tip |** *Laura and Cristina of DuWop recommend you curl your lashes before applying water proof mascara. Brunettes can use the mascara to cover up stray grays.*

✳ **Anti-Bride Tip |** *To keep makeup lasting all night, spray a brush or powder puff with hairspray before dipping into powder, says Diane Irons.*

✳ From San Francisco Dermatologist Dr. Vail Reese:

Dr. Reese recommends that if you don't already have a trusted and true dermatologist, ask your friends and primary physician for referrals. Also, check out the American Academy of Dermatology Web site at *www.aad.org*. On your first visit, make sure you're comfortable with the office and the dermatologist's style. And double check that he or she has experience with medical and cosmetic treatments, just in case you need a bit of both. If the doctor doesn't fully explain procedures or answer questions or pushes cosmetic procedures or excessive products, keep shopping around. When you should see your dermatologist depends on the medical or cosmetic issues. In general, it's a good idea to meet with your dermatologist at least a year before your wedding.

Use gentle, natural cleansers; simple moisturizers like those from Sundari (*www.sundari.com*); and sunscreens (especially ones with zinc for long-term exposure). Since the sun worsens everything from wrinkles to sunspots, stay protected before and after the wedding and on the honeymoon.

Glycolic acid products may be of some benefit, but keep it simple. If a regimen works in the months before the nuptial, don't try something different just before. That new peel or mask may be more trouble than it's worth.

✳ **Anti-Bride Tip |** *Hot oil treatments make for the silkiest hair. Try this at home: Warm a hot oil packet in a glass of hot water, put oil in your hair, and wrap hair in a plastic bag. Have a glass of wine in the tub, and wait 30 minutes. Wash hair as usual—your hair is now pure silk.*

Beauty Appointments

Use these worksheets to keep track of your beauty appointments.

Hairstyling

Stylist: _____ Salon: _____

Address: _____

Phone: _____ Hours: _____

Consultations: _____

Date: _____ Time: _____

Date: _____ Time: _____

Date: _____ Time: _____

Wedding Day Appointment: _____

Location: _____

Date: _____ Time: _____

Total Cost: _____ O/T Cost: _____

{Paste hair pics and ideas here}

{Paste hair pics and ideas here}

Beauty Appointments

Manicurist

Name: _____ Salon: _____

Address: _____

Phone: _____ Hours: _____

Wedding Day Appointment: _____

Location: _____

Date: _____ Time: _____

Total Cost: _____ O/T Cost: _____

Makeup

Artist: _____ Salon: _____

Address: _____

Phone: _____ Hours: _____

Consultations: _____

Date: _____ Time: _____

Wedding Day Appointment: _____

Location: _____

Date: _____ Time: _____

Total Cost: _____ O/T Cost: _____

91

Beauty Appointments

Spa Treatments

Salon:

Address:

Phone: Hours:

Consultations:

Date: Time:

Date: Time:

Date: Time:

Total Cost: O/T Cost:

Dermatologist

Doctor:

Address:

Phone: Hours:

Consultations:

Date: Time:

Date: Time:

Date: Time:

Total Cost: O/T Cost:

Notes

Notes

Notes

Notes

Chapter 8

Dressed to Thrill

{Donning your Anti-Bride attire}

Have you seen a gal walk into a room in a dress that defies description—and the necklace, heels, and handbag all work even if they don't match? That's style. There's a certain savoir-faire and lovely reck-lessness that comes with true chic: Coco Chanel had it, as did Elsa Schiaparelli and Audrey and Katharine Hepburn. These women turned their well-heeled feet in the opposite direction of whatever the fashion press was doing. Using the guidelines to veer off the well-trod path is the key, and you, dear Anti-Bride, can make you and your bridesmaids' fashion mark this way.

Many brides and bridesmaids are happy to plunk down a reasonable fee for a dress they'll wear again. For example, bridesmaids' dresses designed by stylish names like Max Azria or Thread often go for $300 or less and fly out of stores. The reason? The dresses can be worn as a wedding dress, as a bridesmaid's dress, or at any evening event after the main event. They come in a range of palettes, configurations, and materials, and they're a little easier on the beaded clutch than a $10,000 Vera Wang. You could use the balance as a down payment on a house! Anti-Brides mix up their color, material, and embel-lishment choices, and have fun with it.

✳ **Anti-Bride Tip |** *Think big, bold-colored stones—canary diamonds, pink diamonds, rubies, emeralds. If you are wearing a white dress, it is perfectly okay to wear a large, vintage garnet necklace. Get away from the "matchy" look of traditional bridal jewelry.*

Anti-Bride Dress Commandments

❋ 1.
Work with your assets.

Know your body shape, height, and coloring, and stick to what shapes and silhouettes suit you. Look in a three-way mirror with the jaundiced eye of a Thoroughbred trainer. The French have a word for how to create a lovely silhouette: *ligne* or "line." Ignoring figure flaws calls attention to what needs work; working with your proportions and shape amplifies what's right.

❋ 2.
Not every runway trend is real-way trend.

Chic is all about choosing your clothes with thought and discretion, and then not thinking another moment about them. It's not about spending a lot of money on a lot of different looks; it's about finding the perfect look for you and being the very best version of yourself.

❋ 3.
Wear the garment; the garment should not wear you.

Nothing is worse than pinching shoes, a tight bodice, an itchy crinoline, or a constricting corset. Comfort is key to truly enjoying your wedding. Choose garments that transform you in gorgeous ways, not garments that ask things of your body that it cannot deliver. Create a look that offers private pleasures: silk underwear, a cotton-lined bodice, shoes you can dance in, a dress that doesn't feel like a suit of armor. You will look more relaxed and glow like a candle.

❋ 4.
Do not ask your bridesmaids to wear something that you would not wear yourself.

Do not ask them to buy something that can't be worn again, or is out of their price range. Do not expect all bridesmaids to wear the same style, especially if they have different body types.

❋ 5.
Wear color in your jewelry; create size, scale, and drama.

Just don't wear everything all at once. Remember when your grandmother said, "Get completely dressed and take off one piece of jewelry?" It's not bad advice.

ANTI-BRIDE DRESS QUESTIONNAIRE

Use this questionnaire as a jump-off point to get you thinking about the dress for you. Carry it with you for inspiration as you shop around.

1. When was the last time you got dressed up and felt like a knockout?

Ed's wedding

2. OK, so what were you wearing?

Red dress, tousled hair

3. What did you see in the mirror that you loved?

Radiant skin, figure

4. When it comes to getting dressed to go out, your attitude is:

☐ *Always dress like you're going somewhere better later.*
☐ *Feather boas are always appropriate.*
☐ *Yes, I can actually walk in these!*
☒ *I can wear jeans there, right?*

5. What best describes your favorite clothing?

☐ *If it's small, stretchy, and black, I'll wear it.*
☐ *A snappy skirt, a tailored shirt, and a fab little purse*
☐ *Well, I found this top at a thrift store, but I cut off the sleeves and added some fringe along the bottom, and the pants were my roommate's mom's from when she lived in Palm Beach in the 1960s . . .*
☒ *Soft old jeans and the perfect faded T-shirt*
☐ *Vintage cardigan, mod pencil skirt, and mules*

6. My bod rules! Or, at least, this part does (go ahead and brag):

☐ *My curves, curves, curves*
☐ *My killer legs*
☐ *My sexy posterior*
☐ *My beautiful arms and hands*
☒ *My pretty neck and shoulders*

99

Pardon me, I Speak Gown

To get what you want, you have to know some basic terms, so here's our quickie guide to dress lingo.

Dresses

Bias cut: *Fabric is cut on the diagonal so it hugs curves—often used in slip dresses.*

> PRO: *Verrrry sexy, in a 1930s-siren, slinky-negligee kind of way.*

> CON: *You can't wear much of anything under a bias-cut dress—even a bra can show through.*

Basque waist: *This fitted style shows off your waist. The hem of the bodice comes to a point at the front of the belly—think Disney's Snow White. The skirt is usually full.*

> PRO: *Adds structure, especially for a fuller figure.*

> CON: *Full skirt can pouf out around the hips.*

Empire waist: *Named for Empress Josephine, Napoleon's wife, an Empire waist is gathered just under the bust, then falls in a slight A-line shape to the hem.*

> PRO: *Flattering to any figure.*

> CON: *Because Empire-waist dresses hide your stomach, some guests may assume you're pregnant.*

Mermaid: *A gown that's fitted through the bodice, hips, and thighs, swelling out into a skirt-shaped "bell" around the knees.*

> PRO: *Shows off a curvy figure.*

> CON: *No room for any lumps or bumps. Best on an hourglass figure.*

Princess cut: *Seams or darts shape the bodice into a graceful hourglass shape from bust to hips, without the usual gathered waist.*

> PRO: *Doesn't chop you in half at the waist; good for a curvy figure.*

> CON: *Can look old-fashioned; heavy fabrics (like velvet) can look bulky.*

Necklines

Boat or bateau: *Straight line across collarbone from shoulder to shoulder; often paired with a fitted bodice.*

PRO: *Emphasizes broad shoulders; good for playing down a big bust.*

CON: *Bra straps can show; wear a strapless bra or merry widow.*

Halter top: *Think 1950s-style bathing suit. Straps hug the neck and tie, fasten, or loop at the nape.*

PRO: *Cool and fashionable; great with a smaller bust.*

CON: *Shows off the upper back, so you'll need to wear a backless bra; shoulders and upper arms should be display-worthy.*

Jewel neckline: *Simple round neckline that arcs just under the collarbone.*

PRO: *Classic and flattering to just about any figure.*

Con: *Not hugely exciting.*

Portrait neckline: *Deep, wide scoop that usually bares some of the shoulder and is surrounded by a collar or pleat.*

PRO: *Makes your cleavage look dreamy.*

CON: *Looks best if you have some cleavage to work with.*

Sweetheart neckline: *Think of the top of a heart shape.*

PRO: *1950s-cute.*

CON: *1950s-cute. Also not for the cleavage-challenged.*

Sleeves

Cap sleeves: *Small, rounded sleeve that covers the top of the shoulder.*

PRO: *Shows off your arms.*

CON: *Not the right choice if you're self-conscious about showing off your arms.*

Sleeves, continued:

Short or T-shirt sleeve: *Sleeve that comes halfway down your upper arm.*

    PRO: *A nice basic sleeve, flattering to most arms.*

    CON: *Not particularly spectacular.*

Spaghetti straps: *Extra-skinny shoulder straps that hold up your dress.*

    PRO: *Dainty and sexy.*

    CON: *Can look out of proportion on a full-figured or broad-shouldered woman.*

Three-quarter-length sleeves: *Tightly fitted sleeves that end halfway down the forearm.*

    PRO: *Covers top of arms. Provides added warmth.*

    CON: *Makes long arms look longer.*

Strapless: *Dress is held up with stays in the bodice.*

    PRO: *Really shows off the chest, neck, shoulders, and arms.*

    CON: *Lack of straps and sleeves limits your range of motion when dancing.*

Veil Jargon

Veil manufacturers speak a jargon all their own. Each slight variation in length, width, or shape of cut gets its very own term, all of which vie to sound the most romantic. Here are a few basics to help you on your way.

Blusher: *Short, over-the-face veil that just grazes the chin.*

Flyaway: *Like the blusher, only in reverse: covers the back of the head down to the shoulders.*

Fingertip: *Falls to hip line.*

Waltz or ballerina: *Falls to just above the ankles.*

Chapel: *Usually measures six to seven feet from the crown of your head.*

Cathedral: *Usually measures ten to twelve feet.*

Monarch: *The longest of all veils.*

THE JEWELRY BOX: FROM THE PROS

Lisa Mackey, of Lisa Mackey Design, believes that bold colors should be used in wedding jewelry because white pearls are "over." Her fashion-forward collection includes a palette of colored gemstones cut into briolettes, warmed up with the rich fire of 14- and 18-karat gold, vintage Italian heraldic clasps. Chandelier earrings are the rage—in pink tourmaline and peridot, blue topaz, and much more. The best part about jewelry like hers: You can wear your treasures after the big day!

Donna Davis of Forbeadin' has done everything from wrapped-wire tiaras with 8mm Swarovski crystals and semiprecious jewels to studded barrettes and bobby pins. She also creates convertible pieces that work as tiaras on the big day and necklaces the days after, and also embellishes handbags and shawls. She once created a garnet wraparound necklace that ties at the back and trails all the way down the bride's bare back with heavier gems weighting the bottom. That's swank!

A GRAB BAG OF GLAMAZON IDEAS FOR BRIDESMAIDS' DRESSES

From Bridget Brown of Bella Bridesmaid

✓ *Pick a color and fabric, and let each girl pick her own dress style.*

✓ *Pastel colors are tough for most skin tones. Try reds, blues, and dark browns.*

✓ *If you have truly picked a dress your bridesmaids can wear again, give something they can use with it as a bridesmaids' gift (a coordinating scarf, a matching purse).*

✓ *Consider pewters, gold, silvers, or metallics for shoes. They're the new neutrals.*

✓ *Choose a dress that can be "transformed" from wedding to reception—like a dress with removable straps or sleeves.*

✓ *Consider a color scheme instead of monochrome. Orange, reds, poppies, and sorbets are great together—and great for tropical destination weddings!*

Wedding Ring Tattoos

Nothing says "I do" quite like a tattoo. Some couples choose to express the permanence of their relationship with matching wedding-ring tattoos. This route can be especially beneficial to those who can't wear rings, including some doctors, surgeons, and even carpenters and mechanics. Although this trend became popular nearly 20 years ago, there has been a recent resurgence possibly due to the sluggish economy and backlash against the diamond industry (namely conflict diamonds).

BRIDESMAIDS' GIFTS

The tradition of presenting small keepsakes to the members of the wedding party is a pretty one, and just as you're not going to make your pals wear some outlandish getup, there's no reason to go all froufrou and give everyone little heart-shaped picture frames. Cruise through your favorite boutiques and see what sassy accessories they've got, from glam sunglasses to the top nail polish of the moment and a pedicure to match. Also take your inspiration from the theme of the wedding itself. For a beach wedding, give fun woven-plastic or straw beach bags and pack them with towels, bronzing lotion, floppy hats, and cute flip-flops. You can even throw in some beach reading material—juicy celebrity tell-alls are always appropriate when you're tanning. Here are a few other ideas for gifts that can be both heartfelt and useful:

* CUTE SILK, STRAW, OR BEADED HANDBAGS, ALL FILLED WITH HOME-SPA TREATS LIKE FIZZY BATH BALLS AND LUSCIOUS LIP BALMS
* GIFT CERTIFICATES FOR MANICURES, PEDICURES, OR OTHER SPA TREATMENTS
* LUSCIOUS CASHMERE OR LAMB'S-WOOL WRAPS IN TONES THAT GO WITH THE BRIDESMAIDS' DRESSES
* JEWELRY FOR WEARING TO THE WEDDING (ALL IDENTICAL, SIMILAR IN STYLE, OR SUITED TO EACH BRIDESMAID'S PERSONAL FASHION SENSE)
* SNUGGLY FLANNEL OR SLINKY SILK PAJAMAS IN A REALLY FUN PRINT

Beth Blake, a former editor at *Vogue*, and Sophie Simmons are the creators of Thread (www.thread-design.com), an innovative designer line of outside-the-box bridesmaid attire. Here is their rundown of the most popular fabrics for bridesmaids:

DUCHESS SATIN: A rich and shiny formal fabric; especially great for winter and more traditional weddings

BENGALINE: A less-expensive alternative to duchess satin; also good for formal weddings

ORGANZA: A light and airy fabric; perfect for spring and summer weddings. Thread often layers organza with contrasting hems and necklines.

GEORGETTE: A clingy, body-conscious fabric; very sophisticated

Bride Dress Sampler

DRESS QUEST

Use these worksheets to help you scope out what's out there. Indicated spaces are perfect for pasting in Polaroids of you and your bridesmaids in various attire and accoutrements.

Dress #1

Shop: David's Bridal

Designer: Oleg Cassini

Address and Phone (315)445-0237

Price: $1150.00 - $1250.00

Alterations included? No

Basic style notes: Beaded embroidered bodice w/ satin pick up skirt, Cathedral train

Corresponding shoes, veil, etc.? No

Pros: Beautiful train and corset

Cons: Expensive, heavy, and poofy

Ideas for accessories:

Paste Polaroid or Sketch Dress Here

#1

Dress #2

Designer: Maggie Sottero

Price: $698.00

Shop: NY Bride

Address and Phone: (315)452-0060

Alterations included? NO

Basic style notes: A-line w/ corset closure, chiffon, assymetrical ruched bodice, beaded.

Corresponding shoes, veil, etc.? NO

Pros: cheap, light material, flowing, & flattering

Cons: None!

#2

Dress #3

Shop:

Designer:

Address and Phone:

Price:

Alterations included?

Basic style notes:

Corresponding shoes, veil, etc.?

Pros:

Cons:

Ideas for accessories:

Paste Polaroid or Sketch Dress Here

#3

Dress #1

Shop: **NY Bride**

Designer: **Alfred Angelo**

Address and Phone: **(315)452-0060**

Price:

Basic style notes: **satin, cocktail length**

Color: **cafe w/ mocha trim**

Variations for different body types?

Pros:

Cons:

Ideas for accessories:

Paste Polaroid or Sketch Dress Here

#1

Dress #2

Shop:

Designer:

Address and Phone:

Price:

Basic style notes:

Color:

Variations for different body types?

Pros:

Cons:

Ideas for accessories:

Paste Polaroid or Sketch Dress Here

#2

109

Notes

Notes

Notes

Anti-Bride Tip | *Cameron Silver, of the L.A. vintage shop Decades, says, "Don' t let your look have too many looks. Take one or two innovative points—shoes, necklace, bodice—and build your look around it."*

Chapter 7

Parties Galore

{Throwing engagement parties, rehearsal dinners, and beyond}

Pre-wedding parties often pile on so thick it's hard to hone in on the big day. We're not saying don't have a ton of celebrations—after all, you don't declare your undying love to the world every day. But taking a deep breath and keeping the following in mind can ease your stress and keep you focused on the things that matter. Bottom line: If you want to have a party, that's reason enough for doing so, but nothing is mandatory.

When planning these parties, be creative. They can range from a simple picnic on the water to a country hoedown to a clambake. Plan a party that's indigenous to your wedding location. In North Carolina, you might have a barbecue the night before and serve grits and eggs for brunch the morning after. Or invite everyone to breakfast at your favorite hangout like a donut or pastry shop.

ENGAGEMENT PARTY

Almost a relic of nineteenth-century society, the engagement party seems to be on a downward swing. Typically, the bride's parents hosted it to announce that their little princess was officially off the market and to socially ensure the groom had better escort her to the altar. These days, there's no need to "announce" the bride and her partner as a couple. Most people already know. If you want to have a party, have one. It could be for Bastille Day or any other event you want to celebrate, and then slyly announce your big news. Anti-Bride calls it another excuse to have a cocktail party, so break out the bubbly!

✳ **Anti-Bride Tip** | *Elizabeth Mayhew of* Real Simple *magazine says that hors d'oeuvres can be time-consuming. If you're planning a cocktail party, it might be better to do a huge buffet of cheeses, crudités, nuts, and fruit. Limit your drink menu. Offer wine, Champagne, and water. Serve everything in a tumbler. Keep to the essentials.*

SHOWERS

Showers are another form of extortion. A bachelorette party, yes, but is it necessary to have both shower and bachelorette parties? Out-of-town friends are going to plunk down a chunk of change to come to your wedding weekend. When you add up the hotel, the bar bill, restaurants, and a rental car, the damage can be up to $1,000. Getting gifts for all of the parties is like icing a pastry. Traditionally, the goal of a shower was to help arm the young couple with useful things to begin their new life together. Chances are you both already own some key appliances—having a shower for the purpose of lining your coffers is over.

Instead, why not try a coed barbecue or a night of darts at the local pub with both the bride and her partner's closest friends? Or a small dinner potluck party with just the 10 of you, an afternoon of pampering and pedicures, or a girls' weekend getaway. One thing we know about Anti-Brides is that they crave time with their friends.

Party Service: Words to the Wise, from Elizabeth Mayhew, Real Simple

Casual get-togethers are cozier and nicer than formal events. Serve food that people can eat while standing or balancing a plate on their laps. Think bitesize and keep things simple by choosing finger food or food that requires only a fork to eat. Buy cold salads from the local gourmet deli, and for dessert, consider things like cookies, cupcakes, and truffles.

BACHELORETTE PARTY

Bachelorette parties used to be considered the bride's "last chance to cut loose" before the big day. Last chance to cut loose? Anti-Brides cut loose before, during, and after their weddings! And while penis piñatas and strip clubs are hopefully a thing of the past, the bachelorette party is about bonding with your gals, not about how drunk and tarty you all look as a group in public. You want to glow, girl! Not have pale skin, bloodshot eyes, cottonmouth, and bags under the eyes. Who needs it? Think restorative: a home-cooked potluck with the ladies, a night at the hot tubs, a spa weekend, or a camping trip will fit the bill nicely. Even a trip to the local bar for an impromptu ladies' night is fun—just make it a week before the wedding. Keep it low-key, and get to bed early! As with most of the pre-parties, everyone invited should be on the wedding guest list.

BRIDESMAIDS' PARTY

Ever think about putting the pump on the other foot? Your bridesmaids have spent a few bucks, bought a cute dress (that we hope they can wear again), and traveled from far and wide, all for the pleasure of carrying your veil. Have an event that's all about them, like a brunch or a picnic in the park. Anti-Bride says if you are going to do something nice, make it count: Schedule a massage therapist or a manicurist to come over, or hire a local chef to cook all of you dinner on his night off (they can be surprisingly reasonable, and most restaurants are closed on Mondays). But, remember, the focus of this event is on your gals, not you.

REHEARSAL DINNER

Even the word "rehearsal dinner" gives us stage fright. Why can't people, food, and cocktails be another opportunity for a lo-fi meet-and-greet? Traditionally, this was the time for both families to meet, with the groom's family picking up the tab. We say everyone should help out with the bill these days. It's more common now that families already know each other, so don't pay big bucks at the swankiest spot in town. The warmest, most memorable events are cookouts, picnics, or dinner parties at home. Make it easy on yourself and have a DIY affair: a sushi station with steaming sake and Japanese beer; an Indian spread with fragrant wine and cardamom ice cream; or a Mexican feast of mojitos, tamales, and a taco bar. Simply get several hot serving plates (rent at a restaurant supply store), call your favorite take-out joint, put the appropriate table decor (beaded candle sticks, silk lanterns, piñatas), and you're set! Hire your favorite local bartender to do the honors.

Who to invite? Everyone in the wedding party (with spouses or significant others), and the immediate families of the bride and groom. Resist the urge to invite your out-of-town guests—it's quickly becoming a thing of the past as budgets and resources shrink. Plus, you'll see them at the wedding. The reason for this party is for your families to get to know each other for the first time or more intimately.

Usually the rehearsal dinner is when you give gifts to your parents and attendants. Avoid the hokey jewelry boxes with the couple's name engraved on them—buy something you would want, and then give it, keeping in mind the tastes of your loved ones. Gifts do not have to match or be the same.

Destination Weddings: Don't Overplan

It's a lot to ask of other people to devote an entire weekend to your wedding, and many of your guests will want to make it into a minivacation of their own. Don't exhaust them with the party-after-party routine—give them a little downtime. You could schedule one event, like a breakfast the first morning, and then let people do their own thing. If you do plan more events, make them optional, says Elizabeth Mayhew.

Party Planner

Use this area to jot down ideas and notes for your various pre-wedding events. When you've made your decisions and reserved your spots, add the final information to The Phone Book at the back of the book.

Event

Preferred Dates:

Venue #1

Name of Venue:

Contact name:

Venue Address:

Phone number:

How many people can the room hold?

Price per head:

Menu:

Dates available:

Pros:

Cons:

Venue #2

Name of Venue:

Contact name:

Venue Address:

Phone number:

How many people can the room hold?

Price per head:

Menu:

Dates available:

Pros:

Cons:

Event

Preferred Dates:

_____

_____

Venue #1

Name of Venue:

Venue Address:

How many people can the room hold?

Menu:

Dates available:

Pros:

Contact name:

Phone number:

Price per head:

Cons:

Venue #2

Name of Venue:

Venue Address:

How many people can the room hold?

Menu:

Dates available:

Pros:

Contact name:

Phone number:

Price per head:

Cons:

SHOWER & BACHELORETTE PARTY BRAINSTORMING SHEET

Lucky for you, Anti-Bride, these parties are usually given for you and not by you. Nevertheless, if you've got a certain style or have something particular in mind, use this blank space below to jot your ideas or requirements (e.g., "absolutely no party games or stripper telegrams, please!"), then rip out this page and give to your gal pals or party organizer.

Notes

Notes

✳ **Anti-Bride Tip |** *Have a wine-tasting engagement party. We know one couple who had a blind wine-tasting party: They brought in a variety of wines from Beverages and More, Trader Joe's, and a local vineyard, had a vote, and the winning vintages were served at the wedding.*

Notes

Notes

Chapter 8

Ahhh, the Honeymoon!

{Relaxing after the Big Day}

Before the rice hits the floor, you are already dreaming of that next phase—your first trip as a married couple. Relaxation, soft breezes, sleeping in, and some romantic time alone. Whether you have decided on a weeklong adventure on Capri or a two-week surf trip in Costa Rica, getting to the finish line with ease is the goal. Your honeymoon plan should flow as easily as your wedding if you focus on the basics: what you need (relaxation, exercise, culture); budget; time constraints; and what you both want to experience. Plan smart; plan early. It doesn't need to be a money vacuum to be memorable and romantic.

PLANNING FOR THE BIG SEND-OFF

✳ SO MANY PLACES, SO LITTLE TIME! WHEN SHOULD YOU GET STARTED? RIGHT NOW! CHECK OUT TRAVEL RAGS LIKE *BUDGET TRAVEL* MAGAZINE, AND GET THOSE WHEELS TURNING.

✳ SET A TENTATIVE BUDGET. DECIDE WHAT YOUR GOALS ARE FOR THE TRIP AND WHAT EXACTLY YOU CAN AND CAN'T LIVE WITHOUT.

✳ TALK TO A TRAVEL AGENT, BE VERY CLEAR ON BUDGET, AND SEE HOW CREATIVE THEY ARE. THEY HAVE THE SKINNY ON LAST-MINUTE OR ONGOING SALES AND CAN OFFER THE WISDOM GAINED FROM YEARS OF TRAVEL EXPERIENCE.

✳ LINE UP ROOMS, AIRFARE, AND CARS, AND MAKE PACKING LISTS. HAVING EVERYTHING "PLUG AND PLAY" IN ADVANCE OF YOUR WEDDING MEANS LESS STRESS AND SCRAMBLING LATER ON.

✳ CHECK OUT HOTWIRE.COM, CHEAPTICKETS.COM, AND TRAVELOCITY.COM FOR PACKAGE DEALS.

✳ **Anti-Bride Tip** | *Once you know your destination, buy a good travel book, and read it.*

PICKING THE SPOT: WORDS OF WISDOM

KEEP IT SIMPLE. Chances are, by the time you're finished with the reception, you're ready to enter a sensory deprivation tank. Remember this as you entertain the thought of trekking through the Australian outback. India, Thailand, sure, but remember, it takes 18 hours to get there. You will be utterly exhausted after the wedding, so it might be wise to save the big trip for later.

KEEP IT RESTORATIVE. Or do go to Thailand, but rest a bit first. You've been through this life-altering event and then, poof! You're off to making more decisions about travel, like where to stay and what to do. When is your poor brain and body going to rest? So, go ahead and book that trip to a distant land, but before you head into another huge production in another time zone, take a few days off and baby yourselves.

STICK TO YOUR INTERESTS. Sure, you've always wanted to go skiing at Deer Valley or white-water rafting in Colorado, but are those biceps in shape? Can you even ski? If you answered no to either of these questions, chances are you probably should opt for something less physically demanding.

BE REALISTIC ABOUT TIMING. If you have only a week to spend, do something that doesn't require spending two full days of your honeymoon traveling. Also, remember that it probably will take you at least two days to recover from the chaos of the last several months of your life, so work that into the itinerary.

THINK ABOUT YOUR CO-VACATIONERS. Make sure the place you are staying at doesn't allow conventions, kids, wedding parties, or film crews. "Bah, humbug," you say? Kara Abramson of Auberge du Soleil in Napa Valley warned that other people's wedding party festivities can "take over" a resort, making those vacationing in the same place feel violated. Auberge allows only couples and no one from the wedding party.

Have Gift, Will Travel

Why not register for a horseback-riding lesson or dinner at the hip restaurant near your hotel? Trip registries are all the rage, says Nancy Bodace, owner of HoneyLuna, a wedding registry Web site for honeymoons. "We create gift registries for couples that contain fun things that they can do on their honeymoon and that people can buy as their wedding gift. It's just like the registry you'd find in the store."

DON'T FORGET YOUR BUDGET. Honeymoon trips range between $2,000 and $5,000, depending on destination and length. Don't cheap out on the frills if possible, because this is the vacation of a lifetime. If $2,000 is all you have to spend, choose a scenic place within driving distance and do your splurging on accommodations and food. For exotic, think close by, like Mexico, the Caribbean, or Costa Rica. Help pay for accommodations and travel with the frequent-flier miles you've earned while charging your other wedding expenses. Avoid peak travel season, and always check airfare out of nearby cities for the best price. Buying a travel package (flights, accommodations, meals) or borrowing a friend's or family member's ski or beach house can also be a great way to save money.

✳ Anti-Bride Tip | *Hit the vintage shops and buy up an armful of colored full slips. Cut the slip off around the hips, and hem. Voilà, you have a sexy and lacy camisole that, when teamed with colored beads and a flower behind one ear, is sassy and chic for tropical climates.*

Fat-Free Packing

Pack light! And leave your pricey jewels at home, including your wedding ring (you can use an inexpensive fake on your trip). Here's a checklist to help you:

- ☐ Little, black knit dress
- ☐ Jacket *(that you can throw over the dress)*
- ☐ Cashmere cardigan *(can go dressy or casual)*
- ☐ Pair of jeans
- ☐ Plain black skirt
- ☐ Sexy sandals
- ☐ Several shirts that can do day-to-dinner duty. A big peasant shirt, for example, doubles as a beach cover-up and an extra shirt.
- ☐ Good walking shoes or sneakers
- ☐ Camera and film
- ☐ Any important medication *(including allergy pills)*
- ☐ Traveler's checks *(if needed)*
- ☐ ATM card
- ☐ ID, passports, visas, and other necessary paperwork
- ☐ A good book *(although we hope you're busy otherwise!)*
- ☐ Oh, and don't forget undies, socks, and toiletries to last you through
- ☐
- ☐
- ☐
- ☐

For somewhere tropical, add:

- ☐ Two bathing suits *(and lose the jeans)*
- ☐ Two pairs of shorts
- ☐ Sexy camisole
- ☐ Handful of bangles or chandelier earrings to funk up your look
- ☐ Cropped pajama pants—comfy, cool, and flattering, as always, in basic black
- ☐ Black rubber flip-flops
- ☐ Hiking sandals *(and lose the walking shoes/sneakers)*
- ☐ Sunscreen

Honeymoon Planning

Check out the Sunday edition of your newspaper for deals, surf the Internet, and ask around. Be a student of travel, and ask a lot of questions. Use this worksheet to help you plan:

YOUR HONEYMOON BUDGET

Airline ticket budget:_____

Accommodations budget:_____

Food and drink budget:_____

Activities budget:_____

Incidentals budget:_____

TOTAL HONEYMOON BUDGET: $ _____

Destination Ideas

10 DAYS OR MORE	5–10 DAYS
Bora Bora, Tahiti	Dude ranch in Wyoming or Montana
Fiji	South of Cancún, Mexico
Bali	Jamaica
Costa Rica	Alaska
Greece	Grand Canyon National Park, Arizona
Finland	Niagara Falls, New York
Austria	Nova Scotia, Canada
The Netherlands	Ixtapa, Mexico

YOUR HONEYMOON RESOURCES

Web sites:

_____

Friends with vacation homes or rentals, and where:

_____

Travel books:

_____

Travel agent in your area:

_____

Time of year?

Time away from work?

Hot or cold weather?

Where have you and your spouse always dreamed of visiting?

_____

What activities do you both enjoy? *(Sightseeing, museums, and cafés? Scuba diving and swimsuits? Snowboards or ski chalets?)*

_____

_____

Honeymoon Tips

FOR THE BUDGET-CONSCIOUS: *If you stay closer to home (especially somewhere within driving distance), often you can afford to splurge a bit more on accommodations and activities. Consider using the frequent-flier miles you've earned while charging your other wedding expenses. Avoid peak travel season for your chosen destination, and always check airfare out of nearby cities for the best price. Buying a package that includes flights, accommodations, and meals can be a great way to save money. So can borrowing a friend's or family member's ski or beach house.*

DON'T LEAVE HOME WITHOUT IT! *Traveler's checks, once a necessary acquisition when traveling abroad, are becoming obsolete for U.S.-national travelers. In most of Western Europe as well as many other countries outside Europe, ATMs are readily available and accept most U.S. networks. It's always a good idea to check with a guide or that country's tourist board beforehand, however, to be sure you don't need supplemental traveler's checks.*

TRAVEL SMARTS: *If you are traveling abroad, check the U.S. State Department's online travel advisory Web site at:* http://travel.state.gov/travel_warnings.html.

HURRY UP AND RELAX? *Don't feel like you have to rush off to your honeymoon the minute you've said good-night to your guests. Spend an extra night in your wedding city, and get a good night's sleep before embarking on the next phase of your journey together.*

SINGIN' THE POSTWEDDING BLUES: *Feeling a little let down after all is said and done is normal. Share your feelings with your spouse, talk about the wedding highlights, and then let yourselves enjoy your vacation.*

Notes

Notes

Notes

_____

_____

_____

_____

_____

_____

_____

_____

_____

_____

_____

_____

_____

_____

_____

*❋*Anti-Bride Tip| *Before dashing off, make sure you have homeowner's or renter's insurance that covers your belongings, including your new gifts. If you don't, increase your existing coverage.*

The Phone Book
Important Info at a Glance

Bride's Attendant

Name: Doreen Palmer

Address: 209 Hoover Dr

(315) **Phone:** 559-4356   *Fax:* Syr, NY 13205

E-mail:

Role: MOH

Dress Size: 16W

Shoe Size: 9

Head Size:

Name: Vicki Ochsner

Address: 3281 Lords Hill Rd

(315) **Phone:** 396-7964   *Fax:* Nedrow, NY 13120

E-mail:

Role: Bridesmaid

Dress Size: 8

Shoe Size: 10

Head Size:

Name: Sarah Cleveland

Address: 134 Minerva St.

(315) **Phone:** 450-8623   *Fax:* Syr, NY 13205

E-mail:

Role: Bridesmaid

Dress Size: 8

Shoe Size: 8

Head Size:

Name: Brittany Leonard

Address: 108 Franklin Ave

(315) **Phone:** 727-0470   *Fax:* Solvay, NY 13209

E-mail:

Role: Bridesmaid

Dress Size: 16

Shoe Size:

Head Size:

Name: Jamie Stevens

Address: 124 Dutton Ave.

(315) **Phone:** 329-9680   *Fax:* Nedrow, NY 13120

E-mail:

Role: Bridesmaid

Dress Size: 18

Shoe Size: 9½-10

Head Size:

Groom's Attendants

Name: Casey Simek   **Role:** Best Man

Address: 521 Stolp Ave

(315) Phone: 882-7914   **Fax:** Syr, NY 13207

Pant Size: **Shirt Size:**

Shoe Size:

E-mail: **Head Size:**

Name: Kevin Hatch   **Role:** Groomsman

Address: 137 W. Cheltenham Rd.

(315) Phone: 882-1479   **Fax:** Syr, NY 13205

Pant Size: **Shirt Size:**

Shoe Size:

E-mail: **Head Size:**

Name: Mark Ochsner   **Role:** Groomsman

Address: 3281 Lords Hill Rd.

(315) Phone: 530-2649   **Fax:** Nedrow, NY 13120

Pant Size: **Shirt Size:**

Shoe Size:

E-mail: **Head Size:**

Name: Patrick Ochsner   **Role:** Groomsman

Address: 3281 Lords Hill Rd.

(315) Phone: 144-3041   **Fax:** Nedrow, NY 13120

Pant Size: **Shirt Size:**

Shoe Size:

E-mail: **Head Size:**

Name: David Hatch   **Role:** Groomsman

Address: 212 E Patricia Ln.

(315) Phone: 572-2679   **Fax:** N Syr, NY 13212

Pant Size: **Shirt Size:**

Shoe Size:

E-mail: **Head Size:**

Ceremony Information

Wedding Date: 10/1/11   Time: 4:30pm

Location: 3000 Erie Blvd, E   Contact: Carlie

Phone (315)445-0331   Fax: (315)445-2769

E-mail: office @ dewittchurch.org

Site Coordinator:

Phone: Fax:

E-mail:

Officiant: Fee:

Officiant: Fee:

Number of Guests:

Readers:

Readings:

Music: ~~Doug~~ Dennis Triggs

Processional:

Ceremony:

Recessional:

Decorations/Candles: Provided   Fee: None

Other: Fee:

Person Responsible for Rings:

Notes:

Reception Information

Reception Date: 10/1/11   Time: 7:00-11:00pm

Location: 6574 Lakeshore Rd   Contact: Ann/Jimmy

Phone: (315) 609-7828   Fax:

E-mail:

Site Coordinator:

Phone: Fax:

E-mail:

Number of Guests:

Notes:

Ceremony & Reception Services

Caterer

Name:

Phone: Fax:

E-mail: URL:

Staff:

Arrival and Setup Schedule:

Special Dietary Restrictions:

Cost per Person: Additional Fees:

Taxes: Total Cost:

Deposit Paid: Balance Due: By:

Wedding Menu:

Beverage List (if applicable):

Cake

Bakery: **Mario's Bakery**　Contact: **Mario or Linda**

Phone: **(315)452-3306**　Fax: **(315)452-3307**

E-mail: ＿＿＿＿＿＿＿＿　URL: **mariositalianbakery. com**

Address: **505 N. Main St., N. Syr, NY 13212**

Cake Description: **round, yellow w/ ivory frosting**

Number of Layers: **3**

Cake Topper: ＿＿＿＿＿＿＿＿＿＿＿＿＿＿＿＿＿＿＿＿＿＿＿＿＿

Cake Flavors: ＿＿＿＿＿＿＿＿＿＿＿＿＿＿＿＿＿＿＿＿＿＿＿＿＿

Frosting Flavors/Description: ＿＿＿＿＿＿＿＿＿＿＿＿＿＿＿＿＿＿＿＿

Delivery Details (date and time): ＿＿＿＿＿＿＿＿＿＿＿＿＿＿＿＿＿＿

Total Cost: **$371^{60}**　Deposit Paid: **$92^{90}**　Balance Due: **$278^{70}**　By: **9/17/11**

Bar

Beverage Supplier: _____ Contact:. _____

Phone: _____ Fax: _____

E-mail: _____ URL: _____

Staff: _____

_____

Beverage and Returns Agreement: _____

_____

Delivery/Pickup Details (date and time): _____

Cost Per Person: _____ Additional Fees: _____

Taxes: _____ Total Cost: _____

Deposit Paid: _____ Balance Due: _____ By: _____

Brand of Champagne: _____

Brand of Wine: _____

Liquor Assortment: _____

Brands of Coffee and Tea: _____

Soft Drinks: _____

Special Instructions/Notes: _____

_____

Tents/Rentals

Company Name: _____ Contact: _____

Phone: _____ Fax: _____

E-mail: _____ URL: _____

Address: _____

Items to be Delivered/Pickup Details (date and time): _____

Total Cost: _____ Deposit Paid: _____ Balance Due: _____ By: _____

Music

Company Name: Music Machine Contact: Marty Santy

Phone: (315)699- DJDJ Fax: _____

E-mail: marty@cnydj.net URL: cnydj.net

Address: 8025 Pickett Lane, Cicero, NY 13039

Items to be Delivered: _____

Delivery Details (date and time): 7 pm - 11pm

Total Cost: $495 Deposit Paid: $100 Balance Due: $395 By: 10/1/11

139

Transportation

Company Name: S&S Limousine Contact: Jim

Phone: (315) 682-1942 Fax:

E-mail: URL: sslimousine.com

Address: 7160 W. Main Rd, PO Box 340, Leroy, NY 1448

Items to be Delivered: Dodge Durango
(16-18 passenger)

Delivery Details (date and time): 3pm - 7pm

Total Cost: $799 Deposit Paid: $200 Balance Due: $599 By: 10/1/11

Photography

Company Name: K Photos Contact: Kristin Bostick

Phone: (315) 691-4512 Fax:

E-mail: Kphotos34@hotmail URL:

Address: 7085 E Main St, Earlville, NY 13332

Moments to Capture:

Time of Arrival:

Total Cost: $850 Deposit Paid: $300 Balance Due: $550 By: 9/1/11

Videography

Company Name: _____ Contact: _____

Phone: _____ Fax: _____

E-mail: _____ URL: _____

Address: _____

Moments to Capture: _____

_____

_____

Time of Arrival: _____

Total Cost: _____ Deposit Paid: _____ Balance Due: _____ By: _____

Ceremony Location

Place Name:

Address:

Contact:

Phone: Fax:

E-mail:

Officiant

Name:

Address:

Contact:

Phone: Fax:

E-mail:

Caterer

Name:

Address:

Contact:

Phone: Fax:

E-mail:

Photographer

Name:

Address:

Contact:

Phone: Fax:

E-mail:

Reception Location

Place Name:

Address:

Contact:

Phone: Fax:

E-mail:

Music Representative

Name:

Address:

Contact:

Phone: Fax:

E-mail:

Florist

Name: St. Agnes

Address: 2123 South Ave, Su

Contact: Paul Daniels

Phone: 475-7275   Fax:

E-mail:

Videographer

Name:

Address:

Contact:

Phone: Fax:

E-mail:

Dress Shop/Seamstress

Name: NY Bride

Address: 429 S. Main St.

Contact:

Phone: 452-0600   Fax:

E-mail:

Transportation Company

Name:

Address:

Contact:

Phone: Fax:

E-mail:

Groomswear Shop

Name: Jims Formalwear

Address: 429 S. Main St.

Contact:

Phone: 452-0600   Fax:

E-mail:

Cake Baker

Name:

Address:

Contact:

Phone: Fax:

E-mail:

Hair Salon

Place Name: Envision

Address: 100 Sutton Pl.

Contact: Nicole Park

Phone: 446-4414   Fax:

E-mail:

Dermatologist

Name:

Address:

Contact:

Phone: Fax:

E-mail:

Manicurist

Name:

Address:

Contact:

Phone: Fax:

E-mail:

Other

Engagement Party

Date and Time: _____

Name: _____

Address: _____

Contact: _____

Phone: _____ Fax: _____

E-mail: _____

Bridesmaids' Party

Date and Time: _____

Name: _____

Address: _____

Contact: _____

Phone: _____ Fax: _____

E-mail: _____

Shower

Date and Time: _____

Name: _____

Address: _____

Contact: _____

Phone: _____ Fax: _____

E-mail: _____

Rehearsal Dinner

Date and Time: Sept 30th @ 7pr

Name: Tony's Restaurant

Address: 3004 Burnet Ave

Contact: _____

Phone: 432-1030 Fax: _____

E-mail: _____

Bachelorette Party

Date and Time: _____

Name: _____

Address: _____

Contact: _____

Phone: _____ Fax: _____

E-mail: _____